# KISSED

# BY A FISH

## BY SALLY SQUIRES

# KISSED BY A FISH

## By Sally Squires

For further information:
G'Day Inc
PO Box 37126
Honolulu HI 96837
USA
ssquires1717@gmail.com
GDay1717@hotmail.com
www.gdaysally.com

This book is dedicated to
Tifu and Casey
two intrepid world
explorers
with a genius for
the art of discovery

## KISSED BY A FISH

I may not have seen a turtle today but
I was kissed by a fish
I heard a splash behind me and made a
little wish
Then lo and behold, bless me, I'd been
kissed by a fish
I never would have expected it, I'm not a
beauty miss
But much to my surprise I was kissed by
a fish
It's something that for most of us in life
will mostly miss
It's not a usual occurrence to be kissed by
a fish
But sometimes, just sometimes a surprise
is like a wish
And once, just once in your life you too
may be kissed by a fish

TAKE CARE OF THE OCEAN

THE OCEAN TAKES CARE

OF YOU

## ALLIGATOR FISH

An alligator fish has a body shaped just
like a torpedo
It doesn't need a swimsuit or even a
Speedo
It has two rows of teeth so it can crush its
food
To expect it to use a toothbrush it would
think is rude
It doesn't have scales, it has diamond
shaped plates
That protect it from real alligators and all
their ferocious mates
It's two million years old and yet it's still
alive
It can breathe air or water so it knows
how to thrive
And can live for 50 years so it knows how
to survive
It can grow to 6 feet and weigh 300
pounds
An alligator fish is not something that
you would take into town

# AMPHIPODS

Amphipods are really creepy creatures
They have exceptionally strange features
They're a cross between a lobster and a
cockroach
But you can relax as they will not
approach
Because they live four miles deep in the
Pacific
We won't see them and that's terrific
They are tiny crustaceans only one inch
long
So down in the deep deep ocean they sing
their song

## ANGELFISH

The angelfish has got the right name
It plays a most intriguing game
Along the reef it can be seen
Keeping the bigger fish nice and clean
It's never scared but is quite brave
The bigger fish their health it saves
It cleans away inside their mouth
Cleaning away from north to south
The angelfish is a tireless worker
Never missing a fish or a slow swimming
turtle
It cleans from sunrise to when the sun
sets
I'd like to have one as a pet

## ANTARCTIC SPONGE

The Antarctic sponge can live for 1500
years and one has and is still alive
It grows very slowly and loves the coldest
temperatures so it thrives
But this slow growing sponge also has a
secret for the health of us all
Scientists have discovered that it can kill
infections that cast a pall
The Golden Staph infection has been
infecting people very seriously
This infection was one that had been
behaving very mysteriously
Scientists had been scratching their heads
to discover a strong cure
And now they have discovered that the
Antarctic sponge is very pure

## ARCHER FISH

An archer fish doesn't need a bow and
arrow to shoot down its insect prey
It can shoot it down with a strong blast
of water shot out in a strong spray
Then it just scoops up the fallen insect
and has a tasty meal for the day
The archer fish doesn't use its shooting
skills on other fish in the bay
It is interested only in eating land-based
insects and small animals at play
They are not expecting to be shot by a
blast of water during their day
So they float above the archer fish or on a
low hanging branch they stay

## ASIAN GLASS CATFISH

You can see right through an Asian glass
catfish
But not because it's made of glass,
though you may wish
It has no color pigments so it's very easy
to see its insides
Which makes it a problem if it ever wants
to hide
You can see all its organs and even watch
its heart beating
It's sort of pink inside but you won't hear
the catfish bleating
Also known as the ghost or phantom
catfish it's from Thailand
It's a pretty fish because sometimes it will
display a rainbow band
You might see this catfish in their rivers
as it likes freshwater
It will have all of its family there including
its sons and daughters

# ASIAN SHEEPSHEAD WRASSE

The Asian sheepshead wrasse
Has a strange double-headed mass
With a big lump on its head and on its
jaw bone too
It doesn't look like me or even like you
That double-headed mass must be a pain
when it aches
As no doctor fish coral reef calls it makes
It could bang its head hard and not feel a
lump
To other fish swimming by it could give a
sharp bump
Its thick lips and strong jaw mean other
fish it can chew
I think I will stay away from it unless it is
lying in my stew

## BARRAMUNDI

Barramundi is another Aussie fish you
may not know
It was named by the Aborigines who had
seen them go
They have a very strange habit that I will
tell you of right now
They start life as a male and then become
a female but I don't know how
They also do the opposite of the salmon's
lifestyle journey trip
Barramundi start in the ocean and then
into fresh water they skip
They can grow to four feet long and
weigh up to 90 pounds
And they like to travel widely up to 400
miles around
As a large-scaled silver fish they are very
pretty under the full moon
When they do their "love dance"
movements they are really in tune

## BEARDED FIREWORMS

Bearded fireworms look like centipedes
but they are much prettier
They are a type of marine bristleworm
but a little less grittier
Their bodies have 60 to 130 identical
segments with white silks
They are greenish, yellowish and reddish
with a pearly white like milk
They have red or orange gills and clusters
of stinging white bristles
They wouldn't be good to eat as they
would taste a lot like gristle
The bearded fireworm is a voracious
predator and feeds on plants
It won't attack a human unless someone
accidentally stands on its pants
So don't touch a fireworm because it can
sting with its toxic bristles
And then the pain will really hurt and
make you want to whistle

## BELUGA WHALES

Beluga whales have really sweet smiles
And they seem to have fun as they swim
for miles
They are so white they sometimes look
like water ghosts
They have a radar station on their heads
but they don't boast
Scientists say they talk to each other quite
a lot
With squeaks, squeals, clicks and whistles
on the spot
Because they talk a lot they are also called
sea canaries
Even though they may smile at you, you
should still be wary
They also listen as they have highly
developed hearing
And can find blowholes under the ice in a
clearing
A cousin to the narwhal they are not
small
About 18 feet long and 3500 pounds in
all

## BLACK SWALL0WER

The Black Swallower has exactly the right
name
Swallowing fish bigger than itself is its
game
It can swallow a fish ten times its mass
Though sometimes that will fill it with
deadly gas
It can even swallow a fish that is twice its
length
Surprisingly it has that kind of strength
But its secret lies in its huge stretchable
tummy
When eating other fish the black
swallower is no dummy
It swallows and swallows and its stomach
gets bigger
The size of the other fish is the only
trigger
But sometimes even its eyes are bigger
than its tummy
And then it dies so it can be a greedy
dummy

# BLANKET OCTOPUS

The blanket octopus is an incredibly stylish fish
It has its own blanket which it carries to look
swish
These fleshy curtains are webbed between its
legs
And it will unfurl them if a predator is biting on
one of its pegs
With the blanket octopus there's a big
difference between the female and the male
The female can grow up to six feet long while
the male is as small as a snail
Surprisingly that means the female is 10,000
times bigger than the male
These creatures are also very brave as they rip
the arms off a man o' war
I'm sure the man o' war notices that it is less an
arm as it is very aware
Then the octopus uses the poison tentacle of
the man o' war for defence
So it will hit other creatures that it thinks are
about to attack it even if it is a pretence
But the ultimate defence the blanket octopus
has is to drop its blanket like that
And swim off into the sunset looking like
Batman without his cape or hat

## BLOBFISH

A blobfish looks just like a bowl of jelly
Does he smell sweet or does he smell
smelly
He looks at me with such sad eyes
I'm sure he is exceedingly wise
But people overlook him and so do fish
Just once he'd like an audience, that's
what he'd wish
He's really a funny fellow with a line of
clever jokes
He even flashed a little grin when to him
I spoke
So be kind when you swim in the ocean,
be kind to all the fish
You might hear a funny blobfish making
you very ticklish

## BLUE RINGED OCTOPUS

A blue-ringed octopus is a sure date with
death
It's full of deadly poison, even in its
breath
So if you should see one near you, swim
away quick
Or one of its poison tentacles it may start
to flick
So stay right away from those pretty blue
rings
Or a blue ringed octopus may think it
should fling
One of its poisonous legs out right at you
A blue ringed octopus should only be in
the zoo

## BLUE WHALE

Blue whales are the largest creatures ever
to have lived on earth
They are extremely long and have an
equally impressive girth
They can be up to 100 feet long and
weigh 200 tonnes
They are as long as three school buses so
they are very long ones
Their tongue can weigh as much as a
large elephant
And yet for all their great size they seem
to be very elegant
People talk about having a heart as big as
a whale
Well this whale's heart is as big as a car -
that's its scale
But the most surprising thing for an
animal of such a huge size
Is that it eats the tiniest creatures in the
ocean and that's not lies
A blue whale can eat as much as 4 to 8
tons of krill a day
And that is an awful lot of tiny creatures
wouldn't you say

Blue whales can live for 80 to 90 years so
I believe
And I am happy to know that they are
not about to leave
You might see one out boating and even
get a scare
As the spray from its blowhole shoots 30
feet into the air
The latin name for this biggest of all
creatures means little mouse
But I think that's funny because this
whale is bigger than my house

## BUBBLE EYE GOLDFISH

Don't pop the bubbles of a bubble eye
goldfish
You could make lots of trouble for this
very strange fish
It has fluid filled bubbles by its eyes
And its eyes point straight up to the skies
It's not a strong swimmer so can't get
away
If another fish or rock was to prick its
bubbles, say
You'll know it if you see it swimming
ahead
By its bobbly bobble eyes and its noddy
nodding head
It might be so slow that it swims like a
snail
But at least it comes outfitted with a
sneaky double tail

## BUTTERFLY TELESCOPE FISH

A butterfly telescope fish is an
exceedingly beautiful dish
Its dragon black eyes are arranged on
stalks and it looks as if it wants to talk
Its gorgeous butterfly tail is a prancer like
an oriental dancer
Dressed in silver and red and black it's a
delight as it comes back
The Butterfly Telescope fish has an
enchantingly beautiful tail
It might have been stolen from a butterfly
who caught it on a nail
It's big and so delicate like a butterfly's
wings it's fascinating to watch as it flings
As the butterfly telescope fish weaves
through the water it swings

## CAMARA

The camara is a very strange creature
It has several uncoordinated features
It has the body of a shark with the mouth
of a crocodile
I guess that means it is well equipped to
smile
With huge blue eyes it's hard to see in the
ocean
And because it doesn't surface it doesn't
make a commotion
Most people have never heard of a
camara fish
Other people think it's a creature to make
a wish
They figure that because the camara is so
strange
Its wish-fulfilling ability will have a wide
range

# CANNONBALL JELLYFISH

Cannonball jellyfish look just like a big
moon in the water
Leatherback turtles often take part in this
jelly's slaughter
The jellyfish is sometimes called a
cabbage head but it is not green
Blue, white, yellow with a brown fringe
are the colors usually seen
The cannonball is the host to a spider
crab so it is very kind
The spider crab gets a free ride and food
and then leaves the jelly behind
This jellyfish doesn't usually sting people
and if it does it is not dire
But it will hurt badly if you ever get its
stingers in your eye

# CHILEAN BASKET STAR

The Chilean basket star is a sea creature
that cannot swim
And yet it manages to get around
wherever on a whim
It climbs on top of sponges and fish with
its arms
But is a very gentle creature doing no-one
any harm
Its mouth is in the middle of its basket
starry shape
And with its hooks and spines its food
meets its fate
It doesn't have an enemy floating through
the water
So it has a happy time creating its sons
and daughters

# CHIMAERA

Chimaera are also known as ghost sharks,
ratfish, spookfish or rabbit fish
They like to live down deep in the ocean
as deep as they would wish
They are so very strange looking and I
don't think I'd like to see
A smiling cheery chimaera looking at me
as I swim in the sea
400 million years ago the chimaera and
sharks were brothers
And then they went their separate ways
other lives to discover
The sharks developed their ferocious
scary sharp sharky teeth
While the chimaeras just have three pairs
of bony tooth plates to eat
So if I had a choice between being eaten
by one of the two
I know which one of them I would
choose, do you?

# CHINESE DEVIL SUCKER FISH

The Chinese devil sucker is an exciting
fish
If it's living in a pond it will start to wish
For another pond that it can live in
After a while you'll just have to give in
And let it wander off on its little legs
Because it's turned its fins into pegs
It can climb by itself up over rocks
And it doesn't need shoes nor even socks
So let your Chinese devil sucker alone on
its own
So it can find its own home and be free
to roam

## CHOCOLATE CHIP SEA CUCUMBER

A chocolate chip sea cucumber does not
taste sweet
So I would recommend that this fish you
do not eat
Though it looks like it would be a
tempting tasty treat
It actually would be quite salty and even
bitter, not sweet
It looks just like it is coated in chocolatey
chip treats
But its skin is like a jellyfish and not
chocolatey sweet
So leave the chocolate chip cucumber in
its home along the reef
Or you might see it eject itself if you give
this fish some beef
It has a most surprising way of ejecting
some of itself
And then regrowing those parts when it
feels full of relief
So if you like chocolate then I suggest
you buy yourself a box
And leave the chocolate chip sea
cucumber alone in its chocolatey socks

# CHRISTMAS TREE WORMS

Featherdusters and Christmas Tree
worms
Both of them look a lot like ferns
They are some of the prettiest fish you'll
ever see
I wish other fish would just let them be
And not eat them for their dinner or tea
With their brilliant colors
They look like no others
Fanning the ocean waves
Combing them for food to save
Christmas Tree worms are a delight to the
eye
If in amongst the coral you can spy
Their feathery fronds waving at the fish
So many colors more than you could wish
Christmas Tree worms are a visual delight
They would light up your room during
the night

## CLAMS

At least one clam is 500 years old
To live so long it must be very bold
Clams are more human than you think
They have kidneys, a heart, mouth and
stomach
So a clam could also get a stomach ache
Clams also have a nervous system too
So they might feel it when they are eaten
by you

# CLARABELLE, CLARENCE AND CLARISSA

Clarabelle, Clarence and Clarissa are
carefully-cleaning cleaner fish
They clean so very carefully as completely
as the fish would wish
They eat all of the parasites that lurk
inside their mouth
And chase away the germs and bugs and
send them packing south
I wish I were a fish I do afloating in the
sea
And then the carefully-cleaning cleaner
fish could come and clean me
I'd float so very still I would I wouldn't
move a muscle
They'd be quite safe inside my mouth as
they cleaned away the fuss-all
I'd smile at them and say: "Gee thanks"
for carefully cleaning me
If I were a fish, a fish afloating in the sea

## COCONUT OCTOPUS

The coconut octopus is one of the only
animals to use tools
It finds two coconut halves and climbs
inside as it's no fool
Then it can roll and roll and roll across
the ocean floor
And it can grasp the two coconut halves
and close them like a door
So it uses the handy coconut for its
transport and protection
And then it can sneak along among the
other creatures and make its selection
The coconut octopus also likes to walk
and run on two of its eight long legs
And when it's caught its dinner it's back
to its coconut as it's time for bed

# COELACANTH

For a very long time the coelacanth was
thought to be extinct
But it was recently discovered because a
fisherman followed his instinct
It was found swimming quietly off South
Africa in the ocean
And its discovery really did create a
tremendous commotion
It's a gentle fish with a quiet and stately
personality
No wonder it's lasted for millions of years
completely free
So now the coelacanth is considered a
living fossil
And the stories about its death we can
toss all
So far we have only explored seven
percent of the ocean
No doubt we will find hundreds more
animals if we have an exploring notion

## COFFIN FISH

The little red coffinfish has a flabby and
spiny body and a black mouth lining
It is a species of sea toad so it's definitely
not shining
It's not often seen as it spends its time
sitting on the ocean floor
And it can walk across the ocean bed like
we walk through a door
If it feels itself threatened it takes in lots
of water
So it looks just like a puffer fish and saves
itself from slaughter
It has a fishing rod and bait sprouting
from its head
I'm not sure if that is the real reason it is
red
Some people think the coffin fish looks
just like a balloon
Maybe they have been too long staring at
the moon

## COLOSSAL SQUID

Colossal squid have the biggest eyes in all
of the animal kingdom
Their eyes are 12 inches in diameter so
they can see like a wingman
Their eyes are so big the squid can see
objects in the dark that others wouldn't
In fact their eyes are as big as basketballs
but play with them you couldn't
Their eyes are mostly made of water
which seeps out when the squid dies
So if you ever find a colossal squid you
will find it hard to find their eyes
Colossal squid are a real mystery to
scientists who hardly ever spy them
For an animal that is the biggest
invertebrate on earth that is surprising
They are hard to study because they live
in the deepest parts of the ocean
If they lived on the surface they would
create a tremendous commotion
The largest of these giants measured
more than 50 feet long and weighed a ton

With a giant creature so big and ferocious
I definitely wouldn't want to see one
The colossal squid's arms and tentacles
are also equipped with sharp hooks
Some swivel while others are three-
pointed to bring other creatures to book
They are as sharp as tiger claws so they
can easily tear open human flesh
So I suggest you leave them alone
because with their tentacles they could
thresh

## COMB JELLIES

Comb jellies are not jellyfish unlike
popular belief
They don't have any stingers like jellyfish
so that's a relief
But they do have a huge mouth and an
appetite to match
So they open their big mouth and
swallow the animal from scratch
They can detect traces of the chemicals of
other fish in the water
So they slide up to it with one thing on
their mind – slaughter
Once it has swallowed the animal it holds
it in place with special teeth
So the creature has no chance to escape
or to hollow or beef
Other comb jellies have tentacles that are
coated with a sort of glue
So that's how they trap their prey and
they don't even need to chew

## CONE SNAILS

Cone snails are the underwater equivalent
of a tank
They are so strong and tough they could
probably rob a bank
They have a hard spiral shell, flexible
treads and a cannon down below
They are also very clever at hiding in the
sand so they don't show
Not only that but their venom is strong
enough to kill a human
So paralyzing fish to eat is not a hard task
for this superman
It has a sneaky tube which is called a
siphon and is handy for hunting
It's also the way it can breathe when it is
hiding in the sand and not grunting
Though their shells are very pretty and
sought after by collectors
The fish inside is not very nice and not
one I want to see as a prospector
There are 40,000 species of different
snails crawling around the ocean
But if they are all as deadly as the cone
snail then that is a frightening notion

## COOKIE CUTTER SHARK

Don't try baking with a cookie cutter
shark
He might take a bite out of you
He spends his days way down deep in the
dark
And surfaces when the day is new
He has 37 rows of teeth in his upper jaw
And 31 rows in the lower
So together he uses his teeth like a saw
Sometimes fast and sometimes slower
He's chocolate brown on top and vivid
green below
Attaching himself to predators with his
suction cup lips
Gouging round plugs out of fish  - what a
fellow
He leaves cookie cutter marks also on
ships

## CORAL

It may surprise some people that coral are
animals not plants
They all look very beautiful in their multi-
colored pants
Coral are so tiny that they are even
smaller than ants
Algae live inside the coral and both of
them advance
Sometimes when coral are stressed they
expel the algae
They lose their colors and the reef
becomes a sad white alley
Coral are important in new medicines for
cancer disease
They are also used for heart troubles and
Alzheimer's unease
The sad thing is that 60 per cent of the
world's coral is under threat
By human activity which has for many
years the coral upset

## CORAL CRABS

Coral crabs are so small that you and I
wouldn't even see them
They live inside the coral and the coral
even feeds them
The coral crabs would die without their
coral hosts
In other words without the coral the coral
crabs would be toast
The coral secretes a tasty mucus for the
coral crabs to eat
And their very special relationship simply
can't be beat
The coral crabs keep the coral free from
dust and dirt and pests
And when something attacks the coral
those coral crabs won't rest
They will turn on it and attack the
attacker even breaking some of its spines
So the crown of thorns starfish will leave
the coral behind
And the coral crabs and the coral will live
together well
As the crystal clear blue ocean waves over
them swell

## CROCODILE ICE FISH

Octopus, squid and cuttlefish all have
green blood
Ours is red if you've ever seen it flood
But a crocodile icefish from the South
Pole
Has white blood like anti-freeze flowing
through its body folds
The other fish can't see it, it's almost
invisible
It feeds not too often because its meals
are divisible
It can eat fish up to half of its size
So its stomach is not too big for its eyes

## CUSK EEL

A cusk eel is not really an eel
Which is a bit confusing I feel
When the limelight from real eels they
steal
They are in fact a pretty big wheel
Famous enough even to squeal
Once the deepest swimming fish not a
heel
And of the limelight it didn't make a meal

## CUTLASS FISH

A cutlass fish is a very sharp name for a
fish
Does it look just like an extra long knife
very swish
Or does it hang out near a pirate ship in
case the captain calls
And needs to use its razor sharp teeth to
bring in his treasure hauls
Its silver slim shape would be quite handy
for an extra skinny hole
It could slide in and out and capture its
prey before it gets cold
It hides below the surface just waiting to
steal some bait
It is so quick it never misses when it
simply lies in wait

## CUTTLEFISH

A cuttlefish is a very tricky tricky fish
It can take the shape of any shape it may wish
It can look like a rock or a sponge it can squish
It can blend into the background of a coral-
shaped niche
A cuttlefish can travel as fast as a jet
Away from trouble it always can get
It will flash fluorescence in rainbow hues
And can even look just like your blue suede
shoes
A cuttlefish is cunning as cunning can be
It's the greatest quick-change artist in any sea
With three hearts, green blood and W-shaped
eyes
A cuttlefish is also extremely wise
But the Flamboyant Cuttlefish is dangerous you
see
It has nasty poisonous spikes as it roams free
When a fish tries to eat it, it lets out a spear
And that poor fish is dead, so dead, oh dear

## DAMSELFISH

A deftly darting damselfish is luminous
blue and yellow
She likes to swim along the reef with lots
of other fellows
She shows her colors constantly like an
iridescent rainbow
And where she goes to find her food lots
of fish will follow
A deftly darting damselfish has such a
happy face
She takes it with her every day to every
single place
She is quite cute and very sweet to
everyone she meets
And always ready with a smile for every
fish she greets
I knew a deftly darting damselfish once
upon a time
She swam so fast I had to say she looked
so fine
I visit her sometimes when I swim among
the waves
She follows me quite slowly to make sure
I'll behave

## DISCUS FISH

Discus fish originally came from the
Amazon basin
Also known as pompadour fish as their
colors are amazin'
So round that they are shaped like the sun
and the moon
So many bright colors: brown orange
turquoise green and blue
As parents they take very good care of
their young fish
They secrete food through their skin so
the babies can eat when they wish

## DOLPHIN VERSUS PORPOISE

You can tell the difference between a
dolphin and a porpoise by their fins
Dolphins have more curved dorsal fins
but neither of them have chins
Dolphins also have longer noses and
bigger mouths than porpoises
But as ocean going mammals they both
have the same purpose
Dolphins have cone-shaped teeth while
porpoises have spade-shaped teeth
So if you have an argument about the two
you will know the facts to win the beef
They both have lungs and breathe air and
give birth to their young alive
Porpoises seem quieter but dolphins
seem to show-off more when they dive
And dolphins seem to gain more public
attention than their porpoise cousins
There's also more dolphins in the ocean
than porpoises by many dozens

## DRAGONET

The dragonet fish can swim in four
different ways
So it keeps itself busy for all of its days
It can burst swim which it uses when
looking for food
Continuous swimming is for fleeing from
another male – not good
Rapid swimming it uses to flee from
other fish trying to eat it
And vertical swimming is for meeting a
mate to greet it
It buries itself in the sand with only its
eyes visible
And secretes foul smelling substances to
make its prey miserable
Dragonets are also sometimes called
mandarin fish
Maybe because of their beautiful patterns
that look very swish
These fish have triangular heads with fan-
shaped tails
The females do as well but they are bigger
in the males

There are many different types of
dragonets and they are all beautiful
All of them are psychedelic and their
different colors are quite useful
There's ruby red, bright blue, green
spotted, gold, white and many others
Many people keep them in their
aquariums because they are dragonet
lovers

## DUGONG

A dugong is also called a sea camel, a sea
pig and a sea cow
It's got so many names but I don't know
how
It's a very special creature as the only
strictly herbivore mammal
Which means it only eats sea grass so is a
very gentle animal
The strange thing is that it is related to
elephants and not other mammals
And it has such heavy bones almost the
heaviest of all of earth's animals
The dugong has flippers that it flops and
they are shaped like paddles
If it was a land creature there's no doubt
it would walk with a waddle
The color of its skin can change from a
brownish grey to green
Because many types of algae grow on its
skin and can be seen
Dugongs have very small eyes and so
their eyesight is poor
But they have very acute hearing and with
their ears can close the door

They are about 10 feet long and their
body is covered in thin hair
And if we don't protect the sea grass for
them they will no longer be there

# DUMBO UMBRELLA OCTOPUS

A dumbo umbrella octopus flies through
the waves with its ears
Flapping them slowly to swim and using
its arms to steer
It loves the very cold water that it finds in
the deepest depths
So it's not often seen at the surface
there's nothing it needs to get
It's quite a cute and cuddly animal and
will do you no harm
But it's funnily shaped like an umbrella
when it opens right out its arms
So if you see a dumbo umbrella octopus
while you are out at sea
It's a real fish, you are not seeing things,
so just let it fly and be

# EASTERN EMERALD ELYSIA

The eastern emerald elysia is a solar-
powered creature
This green sea slug has an enormously
clever feature
It eats green algae and instead of
digesting it all
It hijacks some of the genes upon which
it calls
By taking the algae's genes it can use the
sunlight
And make food for itself all day but not
at night
So then it can photosynthesize like a
plant does with ease
And its ability might be adopted to treat
human disease

# ECCENTRIC SAND DOLLAR

I wonder if you could spend an eccentric
sand dollar
Or even save it in your bank account for
use as a scholar
What would you be able to buy with one
such fishy creature
It looks quite cute with a flattened shape
as its main marine feature
A cousin to the sea urchin but without
those sharply spines
A sand dollar in your pocket would make
you feel so fine
A piggy bank for sand dollars would be a
thing to keep
And when you go back to the beach you
could buy fish from the deep

## EDIBLE SEA CUCUMBER

Would you include some edible sea
cucumber in your green salad for dinner
Perhaps it would turn your tasty salad
into a real dinner winner
They crawl across the ocean floor
cleaning up the place
So that other animals can follow them
across the nice clean space
They look quite harmless and rather
sweet as they slowly inch along
The other animals don't mind them as
they clearly belong
They make clean sand as they go along
chewing up the floor
And spitting out the sand so the ocean
floor will always have more

## ELECTRIC EEL

The electric eel is a sparkling fish
Full of electricity as much as you would
wish
If I find one swimming in the sea
Can I get some help from him for me
Can I plug into him my electric guitar
And when I'm older, my electric car
I wonder if he makes it light as he floats
right through the ocean
Does he make it bright for all the fish in
an electrical commotion
An electric eel would be a treat
With power flowing right through to its
feet
Isn't it a pity that electric eels don't light
up the city

## ELEPHANTNOSE FISH

The elephantnose fish surprisingly looks
just like a bird
But its nose is shaped like an elephant or
so I've heard
It uses its nose for many things including
finding food
It sends out electric impulses which don't
sound too good
Like an elephant in the jungle it holds its
food in its nose
And then drops it inside its mouth just
like a garden hose
It is a peaceful fish but sometimes can be
a bully
With two of them one can bully the other
fully

## EXQUISITE URCHIN

The exquisite urchin is a beautiful fish
that was only discovered by accident
recently
It had hardly ever been seen in fact it had
been seen only very infrequently
It is a rainbow of colors with long curved
spines banded in red and green
And has large purple segments with wavy
lavender lines that people have seen
And then this urchin has some areas with
olive or light brown colors
Some people say that they have seen pink
and white stripes in others
They are found off the coast of New
Caledonia in the Pacific Ocean
And when they were first discovered
being sold scientists had no notion
They hadn't worked out a name for them
because they'd never seen them
So they had to study them to learn about
this new unusual colorful gem

# FALSE CAT SHARK

A false cat shark has been named for
something that it is not
It's not a cat nor even a false one or
anything that's hot
It's also called a sofa shark but it's also
not a sofa
So what it is is not so obvious but it's
definitely not a gopher
It's the only one of its family and so it
hunts alone
It's not even wanted by fishers anywhere
so it's left alone to roam
The false cat shark has a chubby face but
I've never seen it smile
Its fins look like a pair of ears if you
watch it for a while

## FAN FISH

Fan fish have extended fins that spread
out like Chinese fans
They are very pretty fish and their fins
almost look like hands
They extend almost all along the body so
they also look like sails
Fan fish are deep sea fish and follow the
seafloor trails

## FANG BLENNY

A fang blenny is a sweet looking fish until
it opens its mouth
It has two very very large teeth which
would send me packing south
It's very brightly colored and has a sweet
looking little face
But with its two very sharp fangs I will
give it lots of space
Its two big teeth are supersharp and sure
to make you wobble
So other fish decide that fang blennies are
not good to gobble
There's only two fish in the ocean which
have such poisonous teeth
So be sure to only watch not touch when
you are swimming on the reef

## FIN WHALE

The fin whale is the second largest animal
after the blue whale
Some of them have been measured at 90
feet from nose to tail
And they can swim so fast they race any
ship like a maritime greyhound
They are slim and slender and can make
the very deepest ocean sounds
They weigh an awful lot some are 100
tons or more
If one landed on your toe it would be
exceptionally sore
No-one is supposed to kill them but
Iceland and Japan do it seems
It's really a great pity that they both have
whale killing schemes

## FIREFLY SQUID

The firefly squid is dotted with light
producing spots all over its body
It uses the lights to attract small fish
which the squid eats as fodder
It's beautiful and can turn its lights the
same color as the surface
So predators find it difficult to see it and
so it stays safe
The fluorescent lights it also flashes to
find a mate
And once it has laid its eggs it dies –
that's a sad fate
It only lives for a year which doesn't seem
very long
But that is the length of the firefly squid
song
It spends the day at depths of several
hundred meters
Some people love to eat the squid
because of its tasty features

## FLAMINGO TONGUE

The flamingo tongue is a small sea snail
Its colorful insides wrap around its shell
like a veil
It feeds on coral which is not very nice
Once it's been eaten the coral is on ice
Though it has pretty colors on the inside
of the snail
The shell is very ordinary colored like a
nail
A flamingo tongue is pink, orange and
black
If you pick one up make sure to put it
back
Its colors look very pretty I know that's
true
But if you touch its poison you will feel
very blue

## FLASHLIGHT FISH

Flashlight fish can see in the dark
They can see the other fish all the way to
the park
They flash their lights around them to
make a brighter spark
Flashlight fish – their bite is worse than
their bark
If ever I need a flashlight I know just
where to go
I'll head straight for the ocean and watch
the waves all flow
I'll keep my eyes peeled slowly for the
fish I want to see
A flashlight fish is what I need
a flashlight fish for me
You might one day be at the sea
And wonder what that flash can be
Is it a famous flashlight fish?
No, it's probably just going to be me

## FLOWER HAT JELLY

The flower hat jelly looks like a very
pretty lady's hat
It's not really a jellyfish though it looks
just like that
And it curls up its tentacles and tucks
them inside its hat
It does that when it is not using them so
what do you think of that
It has such pretty stripes that you might
even think of wearing one
And though its tentacles are lovely and
lustrous its sting would be no fun
Its tentacles are multi-colored and look
like a round rainbow
And its bell is translucent with curvy
stripes like a special show
The flower hat jelly doesn't live very long
in fact only a few months
During that time it stings little fish and
then it goes Crunch

## FLYING FISH

Why do flying fish fly?
Do they want to live in the sky?
Their wing-like fins allow them gliding
flight
This is a very good way to escape a fight
The ancient Greeks thought they were
flying onto land to sleep
But even today the flying fish their secrets
they keep
Even the fish's body has adapted for
flight
They fold their wings when they want to
alight
But they can also skim on the water to
take off again
Their actions were studied and copied by
early flying men

# FOOTBALL FISH

A football fish you can't use in a game
It's shaped like a globe, it has the right
name
With a lantern on its head it looks very
strange
It waves it around other fish to engage
Then gobbles them down with its needle
sharp teeth
Its prickly bumpy skin make it look like
the reef
The male hitches a ride on the female it's
true
And she feeds him forever for her whole
life through

## FOUR-EYED FISH

A four-eyed fish is a surprising dish
Well it's not really four eyes though it
probably would wish
Its eyes are divided into an upper and
lower pair
So it can see in the sea and it can see in
the air
How tricky is that I know you are
thinking that's so
This four-eyed fish will always know just
where to go
It will never be surprised by another fish's
bite
It can see in the daytime and also at night

# FOX FACE RABBIT FISH

The fox face rabbit fish has only one wish
To eat all the algae but none of the fish
It looks like a very strange combination
Of a fox's face and a rabbit's jaw motion
It helps out the reef with its love for the
algae
It eats the plants that clog the coral in the
sea
The Great Barrier Reef will be one reef it
helps
To come back to good health and not be
clouded with kelp
It's lucky the rabbit fish is so very hungry
That it eats all the algae, other plants and
sundry
Because it is poison so other fish stay
away
And let the fox face rabbit fish hold sway

## FRESHWATER WHIPRAY

The freshwater whipray is one of the
world's biggest freshwater fish
It's a huge ray reaching up to 17 feet wide
– quite a swish fish
But it's really a mystery – only 10 of them
have ever been caught
So all the facts about this big ray cannot
yet be taught
The sandy bottoms of rivers are liked by
this ray
which has an electro sensory system to
find its prey
No one even knew about it until 30 years
ago
So they are still learning about its habits
don't you know

## FRILLED SHARK

The frilled shark is a study in frills
It might even give you some thrills
When you look at its pretty red gills
But its curling teeth will give you the
chills
300 teeth in 25 rows each shaped like a
trident
So they curl and they bend and look quite
bent
Its shape is like an eel or a firey sea
serpent
It takes 3 and a half years to have an
infant

## FROGFISH

A frogfish has a face that only a mother
could love
Or maybe an angel looking down from
above
It has bumply lumply skin all over itself
So it hides on the reef behind a rocky
stone shelf
It comes out to feed and manages to hide
Until a fish comes too close and wanders
inside
That fish is surprised to be eaten alive
By a sedentary frogfish full of surprise

## GHOST FISH

An unknown ghostly white fish has just
been discovered
And this sea ghost broke an ocean record
like no other
It was discovered in the deepest part of
the ocean
And at 27,000 feet deep it created a
commotion
It was the deepest living fish ever seen by
humans
And its species is strange so it looks like a
new one
It has fins just like wings which wave
through the deep
And a long tail fin that gently sways as it
sweeps

## GHOST OCTOPUS

Do you think Caspar the Friendly Ghost
has been hanging out in the ocean
There's a newly discovered ghost octopus
which is causing a great commotion
It's a very cute little creature and is quite
adorable to look at
It's been compared to cute cuddly pets
especially to your favorite cat
This new species was way down deep
about 2.6 miles on the ocean floor
So there's no chance that you will find
this cute little creature knocking on your
door
It has few muscles and is mostly jelly
because there's not much food down
there
It's ghostly white because it has no
pigment in its little octopus body and no
hair
Down in the deep there is little light so its
eyes are used to see light in other fish
It was found recently in the ocean off the
islands of Hawaii the very best place to
live

# GIANT BARREL SPONGE

The giant barrel sponge can live for more
than 2000 years
More than 6 feet across it's much wider
than between our ears
It is a nice comfy home for other ocean
creatures
like crabs and fish and gobies and lots of
other species
Attached to the reef so it cannot move
Once it is there it gets into its groove
It filters water through its body wall
And finds its food and oxygen and all
So if you're out swimming and you see a
giant sponge
Be kind to it and leave it alone, please do
not plunge

## GIANT ELEPHANT SEALS

Giant elephant seals can make a person
look really small
If they were to stand straight up they
could reach 20 feet tall
And if one were to fall on you you'd be
terrifically sore
Because they can weigh up to 4,000
pounds or more
They are excellent swimmers and can
hold their breathe for more than an hour
And they are also fast movers on land
even if the rain comes down in showers

## GIANT ISOPOD

A giant isopod in a Japanese aquarium
refused to eat for 5 years
If I were that isopod's mother I would
have been reduced to tears
I am amazed that the giant isopod didn't
die
After five years I'd be so hungry I would
sadly cry
But this creature lives in a constant state
of hibernation
So you don't need to feel a state of
consternation
The giant isopod lives on the bottom of
the ocean
Where the water is so cold you can't even
have a notion
It looks like a crab but it is much bigger
It can roll into a ball like a mystery figure
The giant isopod is strange indeed as it
swims upside down
Such a clever trick it uses for predators to
confound

# GIANT LARVACEANS

Giant larvaceans are not so big that they
are unaffected by our pollution
These tiny plankton animals are filter
feeders and not the pollution solution
They collect and consume our plastic
garbage which we drop into the ocean
And eat our micro plastic beads which
looks like food in its motion
And then they excrete all these
microbeads onto the ocean floor
Where every year our plastic pollution
increases more and more
What makes us so careless that we would
have such a notion
To think that all the plastic we deposit
will somehow not affect the ocean
Our rubbish does not disappear as if by
magic means
It affects all the creatures in all the
oceans, rivers and streams
We must take care and realize that we
humans need to clean
The oceans, rivers, streams and land and
do what we say we mean

## GIANT PACIFIC OCTOPUS

A giant Pacific octopus lives most of its
life alone
It's probably a good thing for it to alone
roam
Imagine getting a hug from such a huge
beast
Or getting in its way when it is having a
feast
It's the biggest octopus in all the oceans
of the world
The biggest ever seen weighed 600 lbs
but I'm not sure if it was a girl
Its arms stretched out for 30 feet which is
a very big size
Imagine if you were close to it and looked
right in its eyes
Octopus are very clever being masters of
disguise
And such a huge creature can get through
a hole of a tiny size
As long as the hole is big enough for it to
slide through its beaky beak
Then the rest of the octopus can slowly
slide through even if it's a tight squeak

## GIANT SPIDER CRAB

Giant spider crabs have legs that stretch
for 12 feet
So they would be absolutely terrifying to
meet
They grow so big perhaps because they
live to be 100
Many people could feed on one if they
were very hungry
Some people eat them which must make
the crabs furious
And some of the tales about them are
really spurious
Though they look exceptionally scary and
some people are afraid
But actually they are gentle and like to
stay all day in the shade
They live in the very deep ocean way
down where it's very cold
Which is probably why they can survive
and grow to be so old

## GOATFISH

The dot and dash goatfish looks like a
Morse code message
It helps other fish feed as they all swim
through the reef passage
You will know them quite quickly by the
beard on their chins
And also recognize them by their dot and
dash grins
They scrape their chin whiskers across
the ocean floor
I wonder why scraping the sea bottom
doesn't make their chins sore
There are white and black ones on the
surface and red ones down deep
But they all like ocean floor dining, across
the sea bottom they creep
A goatfish is an old fish known to Caesar
in Rome
They wander through many oceans
because they love to roam
They can change often their color but
never their shape
Have you ever had a dot and dash
goatfish lying flat on your plate

## GOBLIN SHARK

A goblin shark has the longest nose of
any fish in the ocean
It also has more than 100 teeth to create a
feeding commotion
It definitely is not a pretty fish with its
long and pointy nose
And those razor shark teeth just lurking
there in rows and rows and rows
I wonder if its mother ever thought of it
as cute
Did its father ever say that its goblin
shark was a beaut
I know it needs those rows of teeth to
find a tasty meal
But if one bit you on your flesh I'm sure
you'd never heal
Because of all its habits I wonder if I ever
should
Change its name from goblin to gobbling
the neighborhood

# GOLDEN MAHSEER

The golden mahseer fish lives way up
high in the Himalayas
It also frequents streams and rivers in
Asia – quite a playa
Many people like the excitement of
catching it as a game fish
It can grow to nine feet long and weigh
120 pounds – what a dish
Its name means tiger fish and it can be
very tough to catch
Many fishers find that with this tiger fish
they have met their match
Sadly our pollution habit means that this
beautiful golden fish is dying out
The increasing pollution of the oceans,
rivers and land we need to do something
about

## GOLIATH TIGERFISH

The goliath tigerfish is the only fish that
doesn't fear crocodiles
In fact it's been seen to eat small
crocodiles and then it smiles
The biggest tigerfish on record was five
feet long and more than 150 pounds
The same size as a super-welter weight
prize fighter with all the same sounds
The goliath tigerfish has an olive-colored
back and a silvery underbelly
But its most amazing feature is its 32
jagged razorlike teeth – what a tally
The teeth are really prominent as this
monster has hardly any jaw
But one bite from this fish would make
anyone really sore
And when those teeth slam down on
another fish it's a sharp clean cut
It's so very powerful and destructive it
does not need ever to head butt
It has excellent eyesight and circles its
prey before it strikes – boo hoo
It is so strong and powerful that it will
slice a 60 foot catfish in two

It's even been known to leap out of the
water to catch and eat birds
The goliath tigerfish and its antics are
really beyond words

## GOONCH

A goonch is a funny name for a fish
It's also known as the giant devil catfish
You might see one if you go swimming in
an Indian river
This mighty big devil fish might give you
a come hither
The goonch likes to swim in large rivers
with fast currents
You might see one swim past you in a
rushing torrent
It's a big fish up to six feet long and
weighing 200 pounds
If you ever see one coming after you try
hiding behind big mounds
Some people think this giant devil catfish
kills people
And so when they go swimming in the
river they are very fearful
It's a very hard fish to catch because it
will sit on the bottom of the river
And you can bet that if I ever saw one I
would certainly shiver

## GREENLAND SHARK

A Greenland shark has lived for 400 years
Scientists discovered this by looking at his
ears
No, I'm joking it was his scales they
checked
They took some off his skin which is
nicely flecked
He's almost as big as a great white shark
At 21 feet and 1000 kilos I don't want to
meet him in the dark
They are trying to discover why he's lived
so long
So they can do the same to humans to
bring them along

## GUITAR FISH

A guitar fish has such a musical name
I wonder if it plays as part of a fishy game
Does it practice its scales when the sun
starts to set
And sings a sunny song, now that's a sure
bet
I wonder if it plugs into an electric eel
And sends its guitar riffs across the reef
in a squeal
Does it have lots of fish friends to make
up a band
And a chorus of seashells singing along in
the sand
I wish I could hear it with its tuneful
guitar
And see it swimming songfully as it
comes from afar

# HAGFISH

Don't pick up a hagfish it's covered in
slime
It's quite a nasty fish, definitely not
sublime
If it slimes another fish it can stop it
breathing
If it covered you in slime you wouldn't
stop seething
It is so very nasty it's called the worst fish
in the ocean
It will eat another fish from the inside out
– oh what a notion
The female lays about 30 eggs which are
velcroed to each other
So all together they develop into sisters
and brothers
It looks just like a big long tube and lives
down in the deep
It's a greyey pinky color and along the
ocean floor it creeps

## HAND FISH

In Australia and Tasmania there are some
unusual fish dandies
Off the coasts in the Southern Ocean are
fish which are very handy
In fact they are called hand fish and why
is of course easy to see
You will see them sometimes when you
are swimming in the Aussie sea
They have distinct hands which have
developed from their fins
And they use their hands to walk across
the seafloor instead of the usual things
These fish are slow moving as they prefer
to walk rather than to swim like the rest
Even though they have fins and the one
above their heads looks like a crest
They have toothlike scales so some
people call them warty anglers
Because they too have a lure as a tricky
way to catch fish with their dangler

# HASSELHOFF CRAB

The Hasselhoff crab was named after the
actor
Its hairy chest and legs was the deciding
factor
It's also known as a yeti crab or a deep
sea squat lobster
So it has several names but it is not a
monster
The crabs live deep down on volcanic
vents in the Antarctic
The males find the mineral rich water
quite cathartic
But the females are worried about the
health of their babies
So they look for cooler water as they are
very caring ladies
They are all very pretty with their creamy
white shells
As they cling to the rocks in the warm
chemical swells
The males grow much bigger than the
female Hoff faces
Because they farm bacteria in their hairy
leg spaces

Then they scrape off the bacteria with
comblike mouth parts
And eat it up quick so it will nourish their
hearts

## HATCHET FISH

A hatchet fish would be a handy friend if
you were out in the bush
With its body shape it could cut through
trees if you needed a mighty push
And if it got too dark while you were
walking in the bush
The hatchet fish could turn on its lights
to give you some extra push
But it doesn't live out in the bush it lives
in the deep sea ocean
It tries to stay invisible and never make a
loud commotion
It can turn on its lights to appear the
same as the water that it swims in
And its eyes point up not down you see
so it can shine or even dim them
It can see up close or far away with its
great big tube shaped eyes
I wonder if I will ever see one as through
the ocean water it flies

# HIGH HAT CROAKER FISH

A high hat croaker fish – does it have a
raspy voice
Maybe it caught a cold and so it has no
choice
But actually it's a music fish as it makes
its heavy drumming
Maybe it is a warning that bigger fish are
coming
Its black and white stripes topped off by
its very high hat
Make it very distinctive sort of like a
mobile mat
It is usually friendly and a peaceful little
fish
I don't think I could bear to put one in
my dish

## HORSESHOE CRABS

I wonder if horseshoe crabs are really
lucky
With such hard shell bodies they should
be plucky
They don't gallop as they plow through
the sand
Looking for food and anything that
comes to hand
Horseshoe crabs have five pairs of
walking legs
Four of them collect food with their pegs
Then they push the food towards the
crab's mouth
And they can do it from north or south
Horseshoe crabs have been useful to
humans for years
As fertilizer and now in medicine to help
stop patients' tears

# HUMUHUMUNUKUNUKUAPUA'A

Humuhumunukunukuapua'a is a very
long name for a fish
It's also known quite widely as a wedge
tail reef triggerfish
It's very brightly colored with blue top lip
and teeth
It has two spines which keep it safe from
other fish upon the reef
A humuhumunukunukuapua'a can grunt
a warning tune
As it scarfs along the reef other hungry
fish to exclude
With its chubby little mouth it blows a jet
of water
It hunts for tasty things to eat or should I
say to slaughter
It can fade into the background or be so
brightly colored
If it's not at all fearful of its fishy sisters
and brothers
A humuhumunukunukuapua'a fish is a
stately fish indeed
Let's hope it will live forever as it hunts
through the seaweed

# ICE BLUE RED TOP ZEBRA FISH

An ice blue red top zebra fish you will
not see on the reef
It's a freshwater fish entirely, fresh water
is its beef
It hides amongst the rocks and doesn't
like to play
It's quite a secretive fish and below the
rocks will stay
It likes to live in water that is clear and
clean you see
So it can find its way among the rocks
that's how it loves to be
The mother is a good one as she holds
her babies' eggs
Right inside her mouth until they grow
their own legs
They like their water nice and warm so it
keeps the chills at bay
And with their blue and red fin looks
happy they will stay

# INDIAN VAGABOND BUTTERFLY

The Indian vagabond butterfly fish
is very stylish and exceedingly swish
Its black, white and yellow thick bands of
color
Give it an Indian headdress look like no
other
A vagabond is a roamer going from place
to place
Not having a home or a part of its own
personal space
It travels in pairs and swims down to the
depths
Not fussy with food but this fish is adept
at accepting what Mother Nature
provides
Each day seeing what comes to it on the
incoming tide

# IRIKANDJI JELLYFISH

Irikandji jellyfish are tiny almost invisible creatures
But their deadly poisonous cells are their most dangerous feature
No one knows very much about this tiny jellyfish's lifestyle
And the scientists are trying to learn about their lifecycle
Only a few centimeters long with just four very short tentacles
In the water they look pretty like spider silk ventricles
But those pretty silky threads are clusters of stinging cells
Unlike other jellyfish these creatures have stingers in their bells
The poison in these shimmering beads is so strong it can kill
And if stung so far there is no known curing medicine or pill

## IRIDESCENT CARDINAL FISH

The male iridescent cardinal fish has a
very big mouth
It incubates the baby eggs in its north and
south
It keeps its mouth wide open to allow the
eggs to breathe
I wonder what would happen if it ever
had to sneeze
No doubt it would explode with a very
eggy sound
And create in front of it a very eggy
mound
The eggs would all be squished it seems
And maybe there'd be some eggy baby
screams
The fish would have to his wife explain
which no doubt would bring her
enormous pain
They'd have to start all over again
And create more eggs like an over-active
hen

Note: "north and south" here is Australian rhyming slang for
"mouth"

# JAVANESE COWNOSE RAY

A Javanese cownose ray
can often be seen in the bay
It's a very strange fish
But is still quite swish
Even though its nose
Is as long as a hose
It seems to have a smile
When you look at its dial
Its body is shaped like a kite
But don't worry it won't bite

## JELLIES

Maybe some of us could learn about life
from jellyfish
They are mostly made of water unlike
many other fish
Like zen masters jellies have learnt to
become one with the water
This is something that we could all take
notice of, we really oughta
Their long distance travel is generally due
to ocean currents
So they allow themselves to float gently in
the soft movements
Many of them are invisible which helps
them hide from enemies
So they continue to survive and prosper
in all of the Earth's seas

## JELLY FINGERS

No one knows where the jelly finger fish
come from
They are rubbery and slimy and some are
two feet long
They don't have eyes or a face, they
simply float about
When they get caught in fishing nets, they
can't get out
They are a jolly nuisance, they gum up the
works
They stop the fishers from fishing, some
think that they are jerks
They've multiplied so widely they are
clogging up the sea
No one knows how many there are or
why they seem to be
They're firm just like a cucumber and
covered in tiny bumps
But some of them have very fine hair and
others have small lumps
They are often called fire bodies as they
can make their own light

An ocean full of jelly fingers would be a
scary sight
Especially as some of them are very long
indeed
They can grow to be as long as 30 feet in
the sea
I wouldn't want to swim and come across
a group
Of slimy long long jelly fingers all floating
in a troop

## JELLYFISH ARE JUST JAZZY

When a box jellyfish injects its poison
into a victim it exerts 550 times the
pressure of Mike Tyson's strongest punch
There is no way you would ever want to
sit down with a box jellyfish to have
lunch
The venom of one box jellyfish can kill a
human in less than five minutes
That is an exceedingly toxic venom the
box jellyfish has whichever way you spin
it
The box jellyfish is one of the very few
creatures in the world with a 360 degree
view
That would be a very handy skill to have
I think and maybe you do too
A box jellyfish has 24 eyes and scientists
think that it can see colors
They also think it can form images within
its simple nervous system unlike some of
its brothers
Four of its eyes are curved on stalks so it
can peer upwards through the surface

Then it can look for the canopy of the
mangrove swamps which is its feeding
purpose
One jellyfish glows green when it is
aggravated so it's best if you don't
aggravate it
The jellyfish may keep swimming and not
notice you as long as you don't berate it
Jellyfish are considered to be the most
successful organisms that have ever lived
on earth
Fossil records show they have inhabited
the earth for 500 million years almost
since its birth
The immortal jellyfish can revert to its
younger self if it ever gets sick
And it can even discard its older body
which is a diabolically clever trick
Some jellyfish can lay 45,000 eggs in a
single night
If I came across 45,000 jellyfish eggs I
would get an awful fright
Jellyfish are so very beautiful when you
see them floating through the ocean

But the lethal ones are not very welcome
because their venom can cause a huge
commotion
Jellies have no head, heart, brain, bones,
cartilage or real eyes, yet they're among
the major predators in the ocean
Their stinging cells are among the most
complicated cells found anywhere which
is an amazing notion

## KISSING GOURAMI

The kissing gourami is a funny fish with
lips just like big plates
It goes around the ocean kissing the coral
and all its mates
It loves to feed on algae and even kisses
that too
The coral all get ready when they see it
swimming through
It's hard to tell the difference between the
girls and the boys
They don't even have the choice of
playing with different toys
They live a very active life and can live to
more than twenty
Of course that is as long as they get their
food aplenty

## KLUNZINGER'S WRASSE

Klunzinger's wrasse is not a big mass
It's a small fish but a very beautiful dish
It has a greenish blue body and lots of
rich red stripes
It gets on with most fish and doesn't
cause any strife
Its home is in the Red Sea so maybe that
is why its stripes are red
It's a well-known sleepy fish and likes to
spend a long time in bed

## KNOB CORAL

Knob coral and lesser knob coral are two
of many coral species
As its name suggests knob coral looks
just like small knob pieces
But lesser knob coral is unique indeed as
it grows a series of arms
And the fact that it's lesser does not mean
that it does less harm
So because of its arms it looks like a
branching tree rather than a ball
And it can spread further than a knob
coral along the reef and rock wall
Both of these coral are extremely
beautiful so they are popular with all
And if you go reef diving you will see
what looks like a rainbow fall
Grey brown cream green yellow and
white are some of their natural hues
Red orange blue pink purple lavender are
also their colors new

## KRIBENSIS FISH

Kribensis fish are very good swimmers
always
They can swim forward, backward and
even sideways
And they are quite fast swimmers for
such small fish
They will even nip the skin of slow
swimming fish if they wish
The females sometimes have a bright red
or purple spot
They flash it on their tummy as a pretty
attractive dot
These fish make very loyal families
especially when there are babies
They form a school and swim together
and sometimes become cavies
When they need to smell something they
suck in some of the seawater
And then they spit it right back out again
in a stream of wastewater
Their body is a brownish color with
iridescent violet and purple
And when their babies are borne they like
to swim around in a circle

## LAMPREYS

Have you heard that some lampreys are real
vampire fish
Like vampires they feed by sucking the blood
of other fish
Other lampreys attach themselves to animals to
get a free ride
These free-riders you may think have got a
colossal hide
Some of the ones which are not parasitic do not
feed at all
They live off the reserves built up when they
were quite small
Lampreys look like eels with scaleless elongated
bodies and a single fin
They are jawless with a toothed funnel-like
sucking mouth to get the food in
I don't know how they can see because their
eyes are under their skin
You might get a real fright if you found one of
these fish in your bin
Efficient swimmers they generate low pressure
around them so they're not in a rush
These low pressure zones pull them through
the water so they don't have to push

# LANTERN FISH

You don't have to go far in the open
ocean to meet up with a lantern fish
There's one lantern fish every cubic meter
so you could meet as many as you would
wish
They are the most populous fish in the
ocean being 65 percent of the weight of
all the fish
And they give themselves up as food to
many other fish as the other fish think
they are delish
They are often confused with angler fish
but lantern fish are a completely separate
group
Slender and silvery with a large mouth
and round eyes they create their own light
in their troop
They have lights on their body and head
and some have lights near their eyes like
headlights
Flashing blue, green or yellow light in
different patterns to attract other fish to
eat not fight

Those living near the surface are
iridescent blue to green or silver,
down deep they are dark brown to black
Deep dwelling ones will rise to the
surface at sundown and when the
morning sun returns they go back
The lights they give off are to attract
other fish but also to communicate with
each other
There are so many of them that on sonar
they look like a false ocean bottom which
is a bother

## LEAFY SEADRAGON

The leafy seadragon father carries the
eggs
It hides them under its tail in a safe little
bed
It shields them and cares for them until
they hatch out
Then it lets them all go with a fatherly
shout
Be safe and take care says the Daddy
Seadragon
Look after yourselves and swim your own
wagon
For the leafy seadragon parents you see
Don't bring up their children at all at sea

## LION'S MANE JELLYFISH

The largest lion's mane jellyfish had
tentacles 120 feet long
It was one of the longest known animals
in the world – so strong
If I ever see one when I'm swimming in
the sea I'll say: "So long"
To bump into a lion's mane jellyfish
would be so wrong
It's a very colorful creature from red to
dark purplish hue
If I see one I think I will leave it alone
and so should you
Or maybe I will call on one of my turtle
friends to eat it
If you're ever swimming in the ocean
make sure you don't meet it
Swim away from it fast because you
mustn't ever greet it
On the other hand you could swim up to
it and say: "Beat it"

## LIONFISH

Lionfish are beautiful but deadly to the
local fish
They move into an area and eat all the
other fish
They are invasive and voracious with a
lion-sized attitude
The way they decimate other fish is really
very rude
The lionfish don't just eat the other adult
fish
They prey upon the babies and that's
what we don't wish
Though their gorgeous fins are really very
beautiful
They are also quite deadly and therefore
not suitable
To get close to a lionfish is not a very
good idea
The poison in their dorsal fins will take
some time to clear
So chefs in Florida are getting their own
back
They serve lionfish to diners to reduce
the great stack

## LIZARDFISH

A lizardfish looks like a cross between a
lizard and a fish
Its skin looks like lizardskin though it has
scales like a fish
Lizardfish are elongated with rounded
bodies and scaly heads
They are often found on the sandy
bottom or on a muddy bed
They are carnivorous and like to eat fish
with their many sharp teeth
They are often caught by fishers but are
not considered good to eat

## LUNGFISH

Lungfish are clever fish because they can
breathe the air
So when the water dries up they don't
have to go elsewhere
They dig themselves into a hole way
down in the sand
And breathe through a tube to the
surface – how grand
They can stay like that for three or four
years
They breathe very slowly so never fear
They'll stay alive until the water returns
And then dig themselves out of their
holey urn

## LYRETAIL FISH

The name of the lyretail has nothing to
do with telling fibs
It's a beautiful fish and really looks like
his nibs
There are so many beautiful colors of
lyretail fish
They come in blue, pink, gold and orange
so swish
Its fins are so pretty it's named after a
musical lyre
The tail is fan-shaped with bright orange
and red flares like a fire

## MANGROVE KILLIFISH TREEFISH

The mangrove killifish can live for several
months in a tree
I never ever thought there was a fish who
didn't live in the sea
It hides inside a hollow which the insects
have kindly made
They feed the fish inside the tree while it
quietly lays
Then each year when the mangrove water
returns
The treefish knows that a water fish is
now its turn
A fish that lives in a tree
would be a sight to see
I wonder what the birds think
I guess they don't kick up a stink
At the fish that lives in their tree

## MEGAMOUTH SHARK

The megamouth shark is a very shy
creature
Its 4 foot wide mouth is its mindblowing
feature
But don't be afraid, no, do not be scared
It doesn't eat humans because the
megamouth heard
That humans aren't tasty, they're not even
sweet
So it leaves us alone and beats a hasty
retreat
It's a very slow swimmer so it wouldn't
even catch us
It has very tiny teeth, no spines like a
cactus
There's only a few megamouth sharks in
the ocean
So don't make a fuss, no, don't make a
commotion
You have nothing to fear from a
megamouth shark
Even if you were to meet one when
you're out in the dark

A megamouth floats slowly like its cousin
the whale shark
Its bite is definitely not any worse than its
bark

## MERLIN THE TURTLE

Merlin the turtle has a very pointy shell
Just like Merlin's hat that we all know so
well
He talks to me often as the waves start to
swell
And brings me small presents and
sometimes a shell
He eats all the algae that live on the reef
Which helps the coral live so they don't
come to grief
He comes up to breathe and will give me
a wave
He's a fearless adventurer and definitely
brave
Dodging sharks and ferocious fish on the
reef every day
Sometimes he will surface and turn to me
and say
Please keep our ocean clean it's our home
don't you know
We need clean water and food so we can
go to and fro
He's a beautiful fish of that there's no
doubt

With a bright eye and a ready smile and
never a pout
Merlin I salute you, you're a wonder of
time
And I'm exceedingly grateful to say
you're a great friend of mine

## MEXICAN BLINDCATS

Mexican blindcats don't have any eyes
So sharp hearing and smelling is where
their talent lies
They live in underground caves so they
are used to the dark
There's no sunlight or moonlight to
provide any spark
With their pink scaless skin they can feel
other fish
As they come through the ocean with a
swishy swish swish
When the males start to fight they lock
their lips together
And can stay like that for hours as if they
were tethered
They are members of the catfish family so
have the same beard
They're a harmless fish so don't worry
they are not to be feared

## MEXICAN HOGFISH

I think that the Mexican Hogfish is a very
strange fish
Though it's born as a girl it can become a
boy if it should wish
It's not very pretty with its big lumpy
head
And the inside of its eyes are a bright
blood red
But its body is colored pink yellow or red
So it has some attractive aspects – well
enough said
Some of them are even striped in a soft
yellow hue
And people love to eat them – oh boo
hoo hoo hoo hoo

## MIMIC OCTOPUS

The mimic octopus is thought by
scientists to be nature's greatest actor
It beats the intelligence of other animals
by an enormous factor
Other octopus, squid and cuttlefish can
mimic the terrain they swim over
But the mimic octopus can mimic other
fish to give it cover
It's considered to be the most intelligent
animal on earth
Not discovered until the 1990s because it
was giving humans a wide berth
One scientist called the mimic octopus
the pinnacle of wizardry
I get the feeling that it is also the king of
devilry
So far it is known to mimic at least 15
other species
That is an enormous amount of
brainpower to mimic so many beasties

## MONK FISH

Does it sit in a cave saying its prayers
Or in a watery room without any chairs
It must be a loner swimming out on the
reef
It can't be a groaner for it can't eat beef
But the monk fish is named for the fringe
all around
Which looks like a monk hairdo when
one is found
It grows quite large and many have said
It lays thousands of eggs into a 20 foot
bed
Which floats through the ocean until they
are hatched
Claiming a part of the ocean as its very
own patch

## MYSTERY WALKING FISH

A new walking fish has many scientists
puzzled
They don't know what it is so they are
muzzled
A diver in Bali saw this strange fish
walking across the ocean floor
It was walking on its lowermost pectoral
fin rays so it didn't get sore
It has bony protruberances off its fins
which have taste buds in them
So as it's walking it's also checking out
tasty fishy gems
The scientists agree that its walking ability
could be the way it hunts
But they can't agree on what it is and the
diver didn't say if it also grunts
It looked like it was going to an evening
stroll across the seabed
It's a pretty fish with silver, apricot and
orange and quite a big head

## NARWHALS

Narwhals have a single tooth that can be
up to ten feet long
They are related to beluga whales so they
both can get along
The tusk grows out through their lip as a
left side canine tooth
And sometimes a male will have one on
the right as well – struth!
Sometimes the females will have one too
but usually it's not the case
But there is a skull of one female who
had double tusks in place
As the narwhals grow older not only do
they get bigger but also whiter
So the very old ones you can tell their age
even if they've been a fighter
Scientists thought the tusks were a
weapon for the males to fight
But now they think it's a direction tool to
clue in others on sight
For marine mammals narwhals have been
recorded making the deepest dives
In winter they can dive up to 5,000 feet
and do it 15 times a day and survive

Like other whales they use sound to
navigate and hunt for their food
Unlike the beluga hardly anyone hears
narwhals and that is really rude
Clicks, whistles and knocks are created
near the blowhole and reflected off their
skull
They also make bangs, trumpeting and
squeaking door sounds but not as loud as
a gull

## NASSAU GROUPER

Unlike what your mother will say a
Nassau grouper does not chew its food
It has such a large mouth that it swallows
other fish whole – that's rude
And on its dinner menu are really large
fish even lobsters and crabs
So when you see one floating in the
ocean it might be ready to grab
I wouldn't get in the way of its huge
mouth if I were you
It might see you as another fish coming
to it as food
As far as I know a Nassau grouper will
never flash a smile
Even if you were to swim beside it for
mile after mile after mile
A Nassau grouper doesn't really need to
ever smile
Even if some people think its look is
quite vile

## NAUTILUS

If you could see inside a nautilus shell
you'd see a golden spiral
It is such a mathematical miracle its
beauty should go viral
These blue blood living fossils really do
have blue blood
So they were around on earth way before
the big flood
Though they've survived for millions of
years they are very modern
Using jet propulsion to swim so their
chamber is always sodden
They don't have a fixed lens so their
eyesight is quite poor
But they can withdraw completely into
their shell and shut the door
It's a surprise to know that they have up
to 90 tentacles
And their blue blood flows to their heart
through four ventricles
Scientists say nautilus can learn and they
do have a memory
Even though their brain is simple they are
very sensory

They are so old that they have seen the
dinosaurs come and go
Over 500 million years they have seen
major events ebb and flow
Maybe they have lived so long because
they take so long to hatch
They spend up to a year in the eggs which
the females to rocks attach

## NORTHERN HOG SUCKER

If you ever see a northern hog sucker in a
creek or a little stream
You'll know for sure and certain that that
river water is clean
For this fish is very careful about where it
swims it seems
And it's also very careful about just where
it is seen
It spends its time in rummaging through
the river bottom sands
Sifting out food from anywhere off rocks
for minute strands
It can even spit out stones from its gills
while it is eating
Which it has turned over to check and
suck off the meaty seating
It's also a good insect catcher with its
noisy sucking motion
But you will not ever find this fish hog-
sucking through the ocean

## NUDIBRANCH

Nudibranchs must be one of the bravest
ocean creatures
Their favorite food is the man o' war and
that is an amazing feature
Not only that but they swallow the man
o' war's poison pieces
And then they use them in their body to
scare off other species
They also are a very pretty sight as they
slowly make their way
Across the ocean floor so colorfully each
and every day
The man o' war is 50 times the size of the
brave nudibranch
So the nudibranch which is a sea slug just
nips away at every chance
It's lucky that this little slug is immune to
the big guy's stingers
Because in its own life the nudibranch
can let go some heavy zingers
As we learnt with that big giant who was
knocked over by a stone
Sometimes the little person wins and that
is a happy tome

# NUTRICULAR JELLYFISH

The nutricular jellyfish never dies, in fact
it is immortal
It has a clever way to live and this will
make you chortle
Every time it grows up big it changes
back into a kid
This is such a strange idea that on it we
must keep a lid
Scientists are really puzzled by the never
dying jellyfish
To keep humans living forever is what
they would wish
I don't think living forever would be a
very good idea
It could get very boring unless you had
lots of imaginative gear

## OARFISH

The oarfish is an awfully long long fish
Up to 50 feet long - longer than some would wish
To have a conversation with such a long creature
Would mean swimming for ages along its amazing feature
It is the longest bony fish to be found in the ocean
So don't be shocked when you see such a long motion
Swimming along beside you as you gently learn to swim
It won't disturb you as you peacefully talk to him
I guess there are some ladies among this long long fish
And maybe they are fashion plates looking very swish
With no teeth and no scales they glide along so smooth
But if one swims beside you, you may want to move
They are a really gentle fish and live mostly in the deep
So don't worry that an oarfish may capture you while you sleep

## OCEAN SUNFISH

A sunfish is a prodigious egg layer
Laying three hundred million eggs – what
a player
It is the heaviest bony fish in the ocean
If it swims by you don't make a
commotion
They're very peaceful creatures they
simply float about
They never raise their voices and never
ever shout
Some sunfish are really beautiful
And others' looks are simply dutiful
Silver and apricot are two of their colors
But happily with sunfish there are many
others
A blue spotted sunfish has bright red eyes
Sunfish really are a tremendous size
14 feet tall and ten feet long like a giant
moon
Their huge body floating like a very large
room
Basking on the surface soaking up the
sun's rays

Their beaky mouths look like they
continually graze
So if you see a sunfish as it floats along
by you
Just smile at it and let it be and you'll be
ticketty boo

## OCEANIC MANTA RAY

Though an oceanic manta ray can be 20
feet across
It eats the tiniest plankton animals
floating in the dross
It often swims along the reef for the
cleaning fish to clean
And it never attempts to eat any of them
as it is never ever mean
It's an eager ocean wanderer well known
throughout the world
And the markings on its back show
whether it's a boy or girl
They are completely distinctive just like
our fingerprints
So scientists can track them as each one is
distinct

## ORB JELLYFISH

The orb jellyfish is a new type of jellyfish
just discovered in the deep Pacific
Scientists found it in the deepest part of
the ocean so that is really terrific
It's a pretty golden jellyfish with red
stripes and two different types of
tentacles
The red stripes are like canals because the
jellyfish doesn't have any ventricles
The scientists noticed that when the long
tentacles are out the jellyfish stays in place
And so they think that is when it is
waiting for prey to catch for dinner in
that space
So they assume that when its short
tentacles are out and its bell is pulsating
That the orb jellyfish is swimming
because they have seen it undulating

## ORIENTAL FLYING GURNARD

The oriental flying gurnard is not a flying
fish
And even though it has fins it likes to
walk to feel swish
It is a most beautiful fish when its fans
are fully displayed
Sometimes it fans them out for fun but
sometimes when it is dismayed
The word gurnard is French for grunt
and that's what this fish can do
And when it fans out its fins the tips of
them are a beautiful bright blue
It has large eyes to see other fish and
maybe to watch the sky
Its body is light brown with orange and
dark spots so it is quite a stylish guy

## PACIFIC BLACK DRAGON FISH

The Pacific black dragon fish looks just
like the Chinese icon
It even has the whiskery beard just like
the famous dragon
It doesn't breathe out fire and smoke but
it can light up the ocean
With lights in its body and below its eyes
creating quite a commotion
It even has a light on a lure attached to its
whiskery beard
To catch other fish by waggling it about
just as they feared
It needs big eyes down in the dark of the
deep
So that during the day it won't go to sleep
With ferocious teeth and an angry looking
mouth
It is something to stay away from – look
out!

## PACU FISH

A pacu fish could eat a great big steak
It has the same teeth as the human race
And though it's a cousin to the meat-
eating piranhas
It's a vegetarian fish happier eating
bananas
People think it's ferocious and decidedly
wild
But in fact it is quiet and even quite mild

## PANCAKE BATFISH

A pancake batfish is a name you'll never
forget
Should you invite one to breakfast so a
pancake you'll get
It might be a trifle batty and fall in the
pan
When you're cooking your breakfast
according to plan
A pancake batfish is a face you'll never
forget
It swims like a turtle and not like a jet
In fact it can walk across the sandy ocean
floor
It uses its mouth like an open and shut
door
It's covered in cones all over its skin
They aren't the kind that you put
icecream in
But when other fish are in trouble who
do they call
They call the pancake batfish who looks
after them all

## PARROTFISH

A parrotfish has a very sharp beak
If ever one bit you, you'd certainly squeak
I saw one just yesterday along the reef
He was biting so hard I thought he was
eating beef
He turned around and looked at me so
fierce
I was worried my skin he would pierce
I smiled at him and waved a friendly sign
And then he said he wanted to be mine
So I bought a big aquarium as big as a
boat
And he spends all day eating as he floats

# PEACOCK MANTIS SHRIMP

The peacock mantis shrimp is an
unbelievable boxer
It's so brightly colored just like a bobby
soxer
It's the owner of the fastest punch
recorded on earth
It hands out a one two punch so give it a
wide berth
Its punch is as fast as the bullet from a
gun
Stay away from this character – I'll give
you the drum
It packs a punch powerful enough to
break a plate glass wall
If ever you are tempted to go close just
give your mother a call

## PENCIL FISH

Don't chew on the end of a pencil fish no
matter if it looks like a stub
For pencil fish like to swim in groups and
create a little hub
I wonder if a pencil fish can write her
name so neat
Perhaps upon a shell or rock – now
wouldn't that be sweet
A pencil fish has bright gold stripes and
even a couple of commas
A pencil fish can leap in the air and do
stylistic bombers
If I were gaily swimming alone upon the
ocean
and needed to write something – just a
notion
I could call on a passing pencil fish
And ask it if it would mind writing my list

## PINEAPPLE FISH

A pineapple fish is not a good swimmer
perhaps because of its shape
So it hides under reefs and only ventures
out at night swifter fish to escape
It's a bit of a stick in the mud not moving
from its perch
You might have to swim down under the
reef if for this fish you search
Just like a boat it has a port and starboard
light
To light its way through the dark watery
night
It's an Australian fish so it lives down
under
Where women are tough and strong men
chunder
It's a pretty fish – yellow and black just
like a pineapple
But whether it's sweet to eat I'd have to
try a sample
A pineapple fish may be good for dessert
If you're on a fish diet and you don't
want to hurt

I wonder how it would taste with
icecream
I better stop now I don't want to make
you scream

## PINK DOLPHINS

The dolphins in the waterways of Hong
Kong are world famous because they're
pink
But very soon there may be no more of
them because the water is starting to stink
Because of all the pollution and the
building of a new bridge and new airport
There are only 60 dolphins left at least
that is what the scientists report
The dolphins are also being crowded by
highspeed ferries every day
So they are starting to disappear
altogether from Lantau Island bay
It seems a fairly small thing that we
should be able to do
To protect these special dolphins who are
still free and not in a zoo

## PINK SEE-THROUGH FANTASIA

The pink see-through fantasia is a
beautiful unusual sea cucumber
It's a recent discovery and truly an
outstanding number
It lives in the deep ocean and has hidden
so far
That scientists didn't know about it being
from afar
You can see right through it to its
absolute innards
It can move very slowly backwards as
well as forwards
When it's in danger it can emit its own
light
It can flash it on or off when it needs to
take flight

## PLANARIANS

A planarian may be a creature that you
have never heard about
It's a freshwater flatworm and what I'll
tell you will make you shout
This little creature has the secret of
eternal life
So it never needs to worry if it gets itself
into strife
If you cut off the head of a planarian it
will simply grow another one
And the new head will still have all the
memories of the old one
Not only that but it has been astounding
scientists doing research
Because it can grow a complete new body
from just a one cell perch
And it is a very fast grower because in
two weeks it will have a new body
And that is absolutely amazing for a tiny
creature that is thought of as a nobody

## PORCUPINE FISH

A porcupine fish is a prickly fellow
It doesn't need to yell and certainly not
bellow
The sight of all those sharply spines
Would make anyone say: Fine,
I'm out of here, I don't like spikes
I'm off fast pedaling on my bike
And off I'd go as free as a breeze
To peddle and swim in other seas

## PORTUGUESE MAN O' WAR

The Portuguese man o' war has venom so
strong it can kill a human
But if you survive the creature's sting you
will feel like a new man
It's not a single animal it's a colony of
tiny creatures
But they can't live on their own which
could be an endearing feature
So they stick together and share certain
aspects of their lives
Which means that they are protecting
each other and so they all survive
There are seven different types of
creatures all grouped together
And a big gas filled bladder which floats
them so they are not tethered
The bladder part is about a foot long but
its tentacles can measure 100 feet
A man o' war can sting a swimmer from
100 feet away - an amazing feat
In Australia each summer the man o' war
stings people 10,000 times

Even detached tentacles and dead man o'
wars can still sting – what a crime
The sad thing is that they are very
beautiful with purple, pink, mauve or blue
ones
But they have to be one of the most
lethal creatures under the noonday sun

# PREDATORY TUNICATE

Predatory tunicates may soon be helping
doctors cure their patients
They could be helping patients around
the world in many nations
The clever way the tunicate's tunic is
made means it has very helpful cells
So they can rebuild our muscles and help
with other diseases as well
Scientists say chemicals found in tunicates
could help cure melanoma and leukemia
So that discovery is creating a great deal
of happy talk in the walls of academia
Predatory tunicates live anchored along
deep sea canyon walls and to the sea floor
Their mouth-like hood is quick to close
when an animal wanders by as it doesn't
have a jaw
They look like a cross between a jellyfish
and a Venus fly-trap fellow
And they are see-through and colored
blue and live up to 3000 feel below

## PSYCHEDELICA FROGFISH

The psychedelica frogfish is a swirl of tan
and peach zebra stripes
It's striped from its aqua eyes right down
to its tail pipes
It bounces like a rubber ball along the
ocean floor
And if you invite it home it might bounce
right out your door
It has fins on both sides that it uses as
legs
So it can walk on the ocean floor quite
well on its pegs
Only recently discovered it hides in plain
sight
To see it hop along on its legs may give
you a fright
The psychedelica frogfish is a shy
creature it's true
It hides in the coral so it won't see you
You could swim along past one and not
see it there
It hides behind the rocks and that's where
it has its lair

## PUFFER FISH

A puffer fish inflated is a big old bag of
wind
He's such a great big round ball you can't
tell if he's finned
His spines all look like harmless dots
But if he stung you you'd be covered in
spots
His stomach is elastic and filled with
gassy gas
When he puffs himself up he's a big
round mass
He's lucky he can blow up so big as he's
such a slow coach swimmer
You can't even see his face so you don't
know if he's a grinner
Puffer fish are poisonous, you wouldn't
want to eat one
If you did you'd feel so hot as if you'd
swallowed the sun

## PYGMY GOBY

The seven figure pygmy goby lives in a
blue lagoon
It swims its fastest in the sea when it can
see the ocean moon
It has a very shortened life, most
unhappily
And after it is born it will quite soon die
in the sea
But while it lives it has such fun it plays
with the other fish
Even though for it a longer life I would
certainly wish

## QUEEN LOACH FISH

The queen loach fish is having a lot of
trouble with pesticides
Rice farmers spread them on their crops
but they don't stay inside
Once the chemicals are in the water they
seep out into rivers
And the poor queen loach fish takes in
the polluted water and gets the shivers
This little fish likes to live in the Ganges
River which is 1500 miles long
But if the river keeps suffering from
pollution it will not last very long
The queen loach fish is a beautiful golden
color with many black stripes
But if the pollution continues it will
continue to be in a great deal of strife
They are excellent scavengers as they love
to eat slippery snails
So they are considered an excellent fish in
the control of those slimy males

## QUEEN PARROTFISH

Queen parrotfish are extremely useful
fish
With their strong beaks they make sand
for the beach
They bite the algae off the rocks and
chew it up small
And then eject the hard bits so to the
ocean floor they fall
By clearing away the algae the coral can
grow
And so the coral reefs get bigger letting
their colors glow
At night the queen parrotfish will exhale a
sticky bubble
At a hole in the reef so that it will not be
troubled
It can then sleep peacefully being quite
safe
And wake up the next morning more
coral to save

## QUEENSLAND BLENNY

The Queensland blenny is something of
an athlete
It enjoys digging and jumping so imagine
if it had feet
It's a peaceful fish and is very definitely a
vegetarian
It likes to eat lots of algae, weeds and
other plants from herbariums
This little fish doesn't have scales as it is
protected by slime
If it jumped out of the water into a mud
puddle it would be covered in grime
When the female lays its eggs it glues
them to the reef
And the male then guards them and
chases away any egg thieves

## RATTAIL FISH

A rattail fish doesn't seem to have a body
It looks just like a head and a tail all
noddy
It's also a very stinky fish with a very
strong smell
If you want to eat one you must cook it
very well
They're not very pretty with their skinny
long tail
But they keep to themselves and swim
slow like a snail
Maybe that is why they live so very long
Or maybe it's because on the deep ocean
floor they belong

## RED-LIPPED BATFISH

The red-lipped batfish uses its fins as legs
to walk on the ocean floor
It has a cunning lure on its back to see
what food it can score
The Galapagos Islands ocean is its
favorite hunting ground
It spends its time on the ocean floor just
walking and walking around
It has a startling battering ram in the
middle of its head
Which it uses to attack other fish before
they have fled

## RED SEA WALKMAN

A Red Sea walkman walked right past me
He didn't even say Excuse me
I bent away so carefully
His spines and spikes worried me
A Red Sea walkman walks very free
He is a sight you won't often see
He's covered head to toe in spines
As I walk – very slowly - behind

## ROOSTERFISH

A roosterfish has a punk hairdo pointing
towards the sky
He combs it carefully every day, he is a
stylish guy
The bold brown stripes on his silver skin
Make him look well-dressed though he's
not thin
The roosterfish is so elegant, I've never
seen one better
He glides through the ocean suavely like
an international jetter
I wonder if he calls out loud early every
day
To wake the fish around him and get
them on their way
Imagine if you ran into a rooster fish
while swimming in the sea
Do you think he would spike you as soon
as he could see
Or would he offer to do your hair as a
punk just like him
So you could have a new hairdo every
time you went to swim

## RUBY RED SEADRAGON

Scientists have just discovered a new sea
dragon called a ruby red sea dragon
It's the first new sea dragon to be
discovered in 150 years so attention it's
grabbin'
Until now the scientists thought there
were only two sea dragon species
This new one is a third and so everyone is
very excited about having a series
In the ocean off West Australia the
scientists caught a pregnant father ruby
red dragon
When they looked they saw that it had
dozens of babies all snuggled up in its
wagon
As well as its ruby red body it has pink
vertical bars on its 24 body segments
To find a new species of a rare creature
like a sea dragon is an extraordinary event

## SALPS

Early airplane designers could have learnt
a lot from salps
When it comes to designing jet engines
they could have had the salps' help
For salps have the best propulsion
locomotion in all of the animal kingdom
As barrel-shaped gelatinous animals the
salps have an intriguing swingdom
Salps are the perfect shape as they look
just like a jet engine
They pump water through their body and
shoot it out the back with vengeance
A single salp can reproduce itself into a
chain of similar creatures
And then one day it lets them all go to
journey by themselves to other beaches
Although they look like jellyfish they are
more closely related to animals with
backbones
And because of their lifecycle they carry
carbon to the sea floor which protects
our homes

# SARCASTIC FRINGEHEAD

The sarcastic fringehead has a lot to say
And it has the lips to say it through, anyway
When two males fight they puff up their lips
And go mouth to mouth just like a kiss
They are such funny, funny fellows
Blowing away just like bellows
The biggest one will puff his lips an extra bit
And the loser's lips inside the bigger fish will fit
To catch their food they jump out and give it a
fright
And then with their giant lips they take a giant
bite
Their bulging big eyes are not so neat
It's very lucky that they don't have feet
Whether they are swimming up or swimming
down
Their facial expression is a perpetual frown
They don't look happy, they look down in the
mouth
When they open wide their giant lips, they
could swallow a house

## SARGASSUM FISH

The sargassum fish hides in amongst the
sargassum weed
This is the perfect place to hide when it
wants to feed
Other fish don't notice it as they think
their way is clear
So they swim very close to it as they have
no fear
Because the sargassum fish looks just like
the weed
Its leafy body parts look like they've
grown from seed
It's green, golden and brown where the
weed is as well
And being one of the frog fish as an actor
it's swell
This fish can change color from light to
dark and back
and it seems to grow weeds on its body
that other fish want to snack
It can even leap high out of the water
onto the weed bed
And can breathe out of water while it is
waiting to be fed

## SEA ANGELS

Sea angels look just like angels of the
ocean
They use their fins like wings in a flying
motion
They are transparent like the angels of the
air
But unlike air angels they don't have any
hair
Sometimes you'll see them swimming in a
kind of dance
Through the ocean waves you will see
them prance
Though they look quite delicate they are
in fact quite tough
And to the sea butterflies they can be
extremely rough
Because they prey upon sea butterflies so
life can be quite cruel
As sea angels eat sea butterflies in a
sudden slippery duel
The problem is that sea angels beat their
wings and swim so fast
That they catch the tiny sea butterflies
who in a race would come last

## SEA BUTTERFLIES

Very little is known about sea butterflies
in fact they are a mystery
They are quite cute and have been around
for a lot of earth's history
Some of them are as small as a pea and
others are the size of an orange
They have two ways of eating but the way
they eat is kind of strange
They create a mucous web much larger
than they are to catch plankton
But if they are disturbed they abandon
the net and swim off like phantoms
They are a sea snail and they have a foot
which gives them their fame
This foot is divided into two so that it
looks like wings which gives them their
name
So they flap and fly through the ocean
like regular butterflies would fly
They are eaten by a lot of other sea
creatures so they do good when they die

## SEA PENS

Do you think you could write a sea letter
with a sea pen standing tall
They look just like old-fashioned quill
pens feathers and all
They are beautifully colored as they wave
in the ocean
Sea pens stand up and their feathers wave
with a gentle motion
But the sea pen doesn't have feathers as it
is multiple polyps with eight tentacles
One polyp forms the stem and holds the
creature in the sand like a receptacle
Other polyps branch out from the stem
and each of them has specific jobs
Some of them are feeders while others
take in water and some form bubs
They are beautifully colored in orange
yellow or white in the torrents
They can move and anchor themselves
somewhere else in the ocean currents
Once they are rooted they can rise up
very tall to more than six feet
Some of them are on the ocean floor
below 6,000 feet like an oceanic street

Sea pens form an important step in the
oceanic food chain
As sea stars and nudibranchs eat them
which must be a pain but everyone gains

## SEA PIG

A sea pig is pink and shiny and has a lot
of legs
It doesn't have a brain and has no
toothpegs
It uses pumps to move its many legs
about
It's hard to tell which is north and which
is south
The sea pig belongs to the family of sea
cucumbers
Its tentacles trawl for food when it wakes
from its slumbers
It lives on the ocean floor way down deep
Like a vacuum cleaner the ocean floor it
sweeps

## SEA ROBIN

With six legs to walk with and fins that
can fly
The sea robin is a strange fish if you see it
fly by
Its fins open and close just like a bird's
wings
So it can fly above the ocean as one of its
things
It lives in the deepest water right on the
ocean floor
And uses its legs to scour the bottom for
food scraps galore
It can sing like a frog as it drums along by
itself
Entertaining the fish that live all along the
shelf

## SEA SLUGS

Sea slugs have such an unfortunate name
They are pretty and delicate and not all
the same
They have frills on their bodies to flounce
when they swim
And it doesn't seem to matter if it's a her
or a him
And as for their colors why they're bright
as can be
Someone must have painted them to
stand out in the sea
I wish I could see them dance their pretty
ways
Every day and every night and all of my
days
One is a Spanish Dancer and that's just
how she looks
You'll see lots of photos in all the best
books
She doesn't speak Spanish or that's what
she said
So I must get this Spanish right out of my
head

## SEA SQUIRTS

Sea squirts have an unusual heart
It pumps their blood in fits and starts
Every few minutes their heart will stop
And then start pumping in the reverse
plot
Their blood is pretty as it's pale green
And it contains vanadium in its screen
Some squirts can concentrate it in their
blood
10 million times stronger than the water
flood
There's many different varieties as they
are tethered
And they are all so pretty and joined
together
Some of them secrete an external mucous
net
Which is called a house and around them
it sets

## SEA STARS

Starfish are now called sea stars which is good
because they are not fish
They can have five fingers or as many as 40
fingers so they are very swish
There are so many beautiful colors in the sea
stars across the world
Some of them seem to be one strong color but
other ones are pearled
They are so colorful themselves but sadly they
can't see colors
Sea stars have an eye on the end of each arm so
they can see others
They have a very surprising way of eating like
no other animal at all
They wrap their arms around an animal then
push their stomach through their mouth ball
Then they digest the animal and slide their
stomach back inside their body
It is a legitimate way to eat and should not be
thought of as shoddy
With such an unusual way of eating they can
digest animals that are bigger than themselves
And so they survive all the threats that come
while they are living along the shelf

## SEA URCHINS

Sea urchins are prickly as prickly can be
They're one of the prickliest creatures in
all of the sea
With their spines they can prick you and
give you sharp pain
You would not want to ever tangle with
them again
They certainly can eat having five jaws it's
true
Known as Aristotle's lantern they
strongly can chew
Not only sharp spines but they also have
feet
More than 100 of them so they can beat a
hasty retreat

## SEAHORSE

The pygmy seahorse is so small it could
fit on your pinky
Seahorses have no teeth and no stomach
so they are not a bit stinky
But they have to eat constantly because
food passes through them so fast
So they eat 30-50 times a day consuming
3000 pieces of food so they last
They have long thin snouts to poke into
lots of nooks and crannies
And they can vacuum in all that food like
toothless aging grannies
When seahorses decide to mate they meet
up every morning for a dance
And they both change color while
through the seagrass they prance
The female makes the eggs but the male
is the one who becomes pregnant
The female transfers the eggs to a special
pouch in the male who stays stagnant
He curls his tail around some seaweed
and dangles there until the eggs are ready
And then he gives birth to thousands of
little seahorses while he floats steady

## SEAHORSES and SEA DRAGONS

Sea horses and sea dragons are a surprise
when it comes to having young
Both the fathers look after the babies
until they are old enough to be sprung
The seahorse mother deposits her bright
pink eggs into the father's pouch so they
can form
Curling his tail around seaweed the
seahorse father rocks until the babies are
born
Sea dragons don't have curling tails so
they are at the mercy of the waves
They also don't have a pouch so the eggs
are attached to the skin on their tails
Every morning the seahorse and
seadragon mothers check on their eggs
And the mothers and fathers do a little
dance like happy little pegs

## SEALS

Seals are very curious animals and that's
why they chase boats
They want to know what is going on in
the boat so next to them they float
Most seals are very gregarious and spend
their time in groups
But the Hawaiian monk seal likes to
spend its time alone as it is aloof
Seals are mammals so they feed their
young their rich seal milk
Seal skin has been known throughout the
ages to be as soft as silk
There are many reasons why seals are
endangered including oil spills
Also the amount of pollution that
humans throw into the ocean can kill
They often get caught up in fishing nets
and then they can't get out
And some are harmed by the boats that
seals follow when they are about

# SHOVEL NOSE CATFISH

A tiger shovel nose catfish looks just like
a spade
It hides in the shallows in quiet shady
glades
It gets its strange name from its
handsome tiger stripes
which go with its whiskers which look
like thin pipes
A tiger shovel nose catfish has a strange
flattened face
It likes to roam widely so it needs a lot of
space
It's not from the jungle in spite of its
name
Eating electric knife fish is part of its
game
You may want to eat one but remember
its size
It may be much safer to cook it in pies

# SIAMESE FIGHTING FISH

Siamese fighting fish are the peacocks of
the sea
They are more brightly colored than any
fish you will see
They have such pretty flaring fans which
really are their fins
They float out around them whenever
they start to swim
There's so many colors of the fighting
fish more than even a rainbow
And some of them are so bright that they
almost seem to glow
If you've never seen a fighting fish then
you have really missed out
on one of nature's wonders about which
people often shout
But a Siamese fighting fish is not a gentle
creature
It's in their name you see this flaming
fighting feature

# SIPHONOPHORES

Siphonophores are long strings of ocean
creatures all strung together
Sometimes the strings are so long it looks
as if something has been tethered
At 40 meters long some siphonophores
are the longest animals in the world
Some of them can be so long that their
tentacles start to curl
The individual animals are called zooids
and they don't all have the same need
So some of them are destined for
locomotion and others are the ones that
feed
Though they are joined together they can
move to different beats
The ones that eat can't swim and the ones
that swim can't eat
Many of them are luminescent glowing
green or blue when disturbed
So if you see one in the water stay away
and you need not be perturbed
All of them are predators and they use
their tentacles to capture prey

Some of them swim for a while and then
on a break they'll stay
A new species just found has a structure
that glows red to entice other fish
And then it twitches like a small
crustacean that other fish think is delish

## SKATES AND RAYS

Though skates and rays belong close
together as family
There are some definite differences and
an anomaly
The main difference is the way they
produce their young
Skates lay eggs and release them in
"mermaid purses" – what fun
The baby rays arrive in the ocean as live
and fully formed
So they can immediately start swimming
as a member of the swarm
Skates also have a dorsal fin but rays have
none or just a little
Rays have thin whiplike tails and a nasty
stinging barb with spittle
Rays are bigger and have plate-like teeth
for crushing food
Skates are smaller and also have smaller
teeth though just as good
Rays seem to be more popular and maybe
it's because they are bigger
But skates as well as rays are both used
for people's dinner

## SMALL TOOTH SAWFISH

A small tooth sawfish would be very
handy
If you were making furniture so dandy
Its nose is like a very long saw with teeth
It could cut through the wood with
excellent speed
Perhaps you could train it to lie on your
workbench
And whenever you needed it you could
wake it with a wrench
And it could saw through the job just as
quick as a flash
And you could feed it on all sorts of tasty
food mash

## SNAGGLE TOOTH

A snaggle tooth looks like your worst
nightmare
And it also looks as if it doesn't even care
Not even a dentist could fix those teeth
It could chew up anything beyond belief
It likes to threaten all the other fish
And doing so it thinks it is very swish
This fish is so tough it can live inside a
volcano
And it can produce its own light just like
a dynamo

## SNAIL FISH

The ghostly white snail fish has just been
discovered
And this sea ghost broke an ocean record
like no other
It was discovered in the deepest part of
the ocean
And at 27,000 feet deep it created a
commotion
It was the deepest living fish ever seen by
humans
And its species is strange so it looks like a
new one
It has fins just like wings which wave
through the deep
And a long tail fin that gently sways as it
sweeps

## SPAGHETTI EEL

A purple spaghetti eel slid across my heel
I got a fright, the eel turned white and let
out a surprising squeal
I'd never seen such a fish, certainly never
in my dish
It's very very shy, not at all a gregarious
guy
Its shyness is a real sin, its eyes are under
its skin
You can't tell its head from its tail
It moves as fast as a snail
It lives its life out of sight
In the sand or in rocks at night
A purple spaghetti eel could be quite a
heel
And never ever feel that it should hide its
feelings real

## SPANISH DANCER

A Spanish Dancer danced by me
She danced and danced so beautifully
She was as graceful as a tree
Afloating in the clear blue sea
I tried some Spanish words on her
Her beautiful dance I did not stir
She whispered as she floated by
I can't speak Spanish so I don't try

# SPLENDID TOADFISH

The splendid toadfish can look mighty
unhappy
He even can sound incredibly snappy
But have you ever heard a toadfish sing
They can do it as well as they can swim
A fish who simply loves to sing
Can't really be unhappy or grim
So listen carefully when you're at the
beach
You might hear a toadfish his scales he'll
reach
Try singing along with him as a tuneful
duet
And enjoy a toadfish song as the sun
starts to set

## SPOTLIGHT LOOSE JAW

The spotlight loose jaw fish could work
as a traffic light
It produces its own light so that it can see
at night
It has two light producing organs under
each eye
But the trick is that one is red and one is
green – don't ask me why
It lives down deep in the ocean at 17,000
feet
So it needs all the light it can create just
to eat
The spotlight loose jaw has a multi-
hinged jaw
Which works for it just like a clever
concertina door
So it can eat other fish much bigger than
itself
It is a very ferocious fish on any ocean
shelf

## SQUIRRELFISH

A squirrelfish is a little nutty
Squirreling around the ocean floor getting
all muddy
Looking for food for him and his mates
Making sure for dinner he's not late
With his big glassy eyes he searches for
food
In every corner of his neighborhood
I don't get too close to his razor sharp
spines
I certainly don't want to make him mine
He clicks away loudly when he sees a fish
And if they don't retreat he throws them
in his dish
A squirrelfish is something that I won't
squish
Because with all those bright colors he
looks really delish

## STARGAZER

The stargazer likes to hide in the sand
It waits for its prey looking so bland
And when a poor fish swims above its
hidey hole
It opens its huge mouth and swallows it
whole
The stargazer's eyes are on the top of its
head
Its body is hidden in its sneaky sand bed
It's not watching the stars or even the
moon
It's waiting for dinner to arrive real soon
As soon as it does it opens its mouth
And gobbles down that poor fish - it's
gone south

## STIMPSON'S GOBY

How about a fish that climbs up walls
using its mouth
It has a clever sucker so it can climb
north or south
It does it by inching and can climb as
high as 30 storeys
It's the size of your finger but can go on
incredible forays
As a baby it starts by swimming in the
ocean
But soon it migrates up a waterfall by this
strange locomotion
It's found on all of the beautiful islands
of Hawaii
To climb 30 storeys would be too hard
for you and me
But this little fish is a game little bugger
With its strange migrating mouth it is a
real plugger

## STONE FISH

A stone fish is deadly as deadly can be
It's the deadliest fish in the wide open sea
It looks like a rock painted in bright
rainbow colors
I'd rather not see one if I had my
druthers
It sits on a rock and watches the world go
by
And when a fish come too close well it's:
"Bye Bye"

## STURGEON

Sturgeon fish have been around for 250
million years
In all that time there's been little change
to their gear
They are very ancient fish and can live for
more than 100 years
That's a surprising number of years for a
fish – so give them a cheer
They are strong because they are covered
with plates not scales
Sturgeon fish are also huge being some of
the largest fish around
Some beluga grow to 18 feet long and
weigh more than 4,000 pounds
A female may release from 100,000 to
three million eggs in one spar
Many people love to eat their eggs and
they call them caviar

## SUNFLOWER SEASTARS

Sunflower seastars have 15,000 tube feet
underneath their bodies
Imagine having to buy shoes for so many
feet – what a hobby!
It would takes simply weeks and weeks to
try them all on
And what a noise they'd make clunking to
and from
They also have somewhere between 16 to
24 legs
I wonder if they ever stop to count all
those pegs
And big! They can be three feet or more
across
Wow! If I met one I'd surely let it be the
boss
They're very beautiful with so many
bright colors
Orange, yellow and red or brown, even
purple and many others
They are certainly more colorful than
your basic brown turtle
As across the ocean floor all those legs
help them to hurtle

# THRESHER SHARK

The thresher shark has a tail almost as
long as its body
It is a very shy shark and is basically seen
by nobody
It spends its time so far down in the
deepest ocean
That almost nobody sees its 700 pound
tail motion
It uses its tail to herd the fish and then
thrashes them
It's a lone ranger and swoops in with
open mouth then
The fish huddle together because they are
so afraid
While the thresher shark goes on its daily
thrashing raid

## TREE CLIMBING PERCH

The tree climbing perch is a fish with a
climbing fetish
Not only that but it can walk across dry
land and not perish
With its air-breathing organ it can exist
on land for weeks
And even without water it will not let out
any squeaks
This fish is strongly determined to get its
own way
It has even been known to hitch rides on
boats to get away
If a bird or another fish tries to eat it this
fish will open its gills to choke it
Perhaps the only way to stop this fish
from invading other territories is to
smoke it

# TRIPOD FISH

A tripod fish is one that walks on stilts
It perches on its fins waiting for food as it
tilts
It lives in the dark on the rays from its
fins
And lies in wait for food like an open
mouth bin
With almost no eyes and a large gaping
mouth
It can catch any food floating from north
or from south
The length of a ruler with fins three times
as long
It's not really a schooler with its long
tripod prongs
Quite enchanting it is with its feathery
fins
Living deep down on its long tripod pins
It uses its fins as hands and as feet
Which come into play when it starts to
eat
A tripod fish should come with a camera
or phone

To take lots of selfies and send them all
home
It's a beautiful fish, an amazing stilt
walker
Leading a solitary life as it's not much of
a talker

## TRUMPET FISH

A trumpet fish doesn't blow its own
trumpet when it creeps up on a fish
It sneaks up very quietly and sucks up the
food as it may wish
When the sun goes down the trumpet
fish is out on the prowl
It is so very very sneaky the other fish
may growl
It looks just like a trumpet with its
strange open mouth
It hides behind other fish as they swim
from north to south
Then it makes its mouth like a vacuum
tube and sucks in all its prey
And has a hasty tasty meal for yet another
day

## TRUNK FISH

A trunk fish is shaped just like a box
And it is covered completely in spots
It's purple and brown with bright yellow
dots
It really has dots, lots and lots
But a trunk fish has a beautiful smile
I floated right near it for quite a while
It finally saw me just floating about
And gave me a huge smile and then
started to shout
I may look quite strange, shaped just like
a box
But I'm happy to be completely covered
in spots
I live in the sea, it's my favorite spot
I'm happy being a trunk fish all covered
in dots

# UMBRELLA MOUTH GULPER

There's a poem about pelicans whose
mouth can hold more than its belly can
Well the umbrella mouth gulper has a
mouth which looks just like a pelican
It's rarely seen by humans because it lives
two miles down on the ocean floor
Its mouth is much bigger than its body
and it is loosely hinged like a door
It has a very useful tail which it uses to
get about and also to attract fish
As bait it has numerous tentacles on the
end of its tail which look very swish
These tentacles glow pink and
occasionally they will give off red flashes
Its tail's whiplike motion helps it to get
about and looks something like lashes
For a creature with such a huge mouth it
has amazingly small teeth to skim
So it uses its mouth like a large net and
scoops up smaller fish as it swims

## UNICORN FISH

A unicorn fish is a vegetarian
No doubt it would like to live in a
herbarium
It's a very curious fellow
The horn on its head is often yellow
It likes lots of company when it swims
But has two sharp blades on its fins
Though equipped for a fight
It mostly takes flight
When it gets a fright

## UPSIDEDOWN CATFISH

A blotched upside down catfish has a
funny view of the world
It sees everything upside down – I might
give that a whirl
And when there's a full moon would it
still look the same
Or would it hang below the earth in an
upside down game
How would you talk to a catfish that is
hanging upside down
Would you have to turn yourself about so
your smile would be a frown
Or could you think of talking to the
fellow's fishy tail
And wait forever for an answer coming
with the speed of a snail
I wonder why the catfish decided to hang
so strange
Does it increase its hearing or give its
eyes more range
Or does it simply like to joke as it goes
through its fishy life
Perhaps hanging upside down keeps it
well away from strife

## VAMPIRE SQUID

A vampire squid can fly through the
ocean
Its fins give it amazing locomotion
Its large eyes can be red or blue
Its body is black or a rich red hue
It lives in the dark as vampires do
It can light itself up like a rainbow too
Its body is jelly like its octopus cousin
Its eight arms have spines more than a
dozen
When it's attacked it turns itself inside out
That's such a neat trick it can flout
Don't be alarmed and don't be afraid
A vampire squid your blood will not raid

## VIPERFISH

A viperfish doesn't need a dentist for its
razor sharp long teeth
It hides in the dark and flashes its light to
catch fish down in the deep
Its lower jaw has a handy hinge to help it
eat its dinner
Able to flash its lights on and off is a
certain winner
With no scales like other fish just a
slippery, slimy coating
It slides through the ocean superfast you
might see it when you're boating
A viperfish is ferocious and has a tricky
lure
It wiggles it off the top of its head
diabolically sure
Its teeth are long and curvy too long to
go into its mouth
They close above its head when its mouth
is north and south
A viperfish is not someone you would
want as a friendly mate
It looks very scary with its mouth just like
a gate

## WALRUS

You'd need a big toothbrush to clean a walrus'
tusks
And you'd need the walrus to stay still and not
fuss
Their tusks are big teeth more than three feet
long
And they can weigh up to 12 pounds and are
very strong
Weighing 3,500 pounds walruses can look
funny as they flipper about on land
It's hard to know how they can get about so
easily as they move along the sand
The favorite food of walrus is clams and they
suck the clam-meat out of the shells
They often spit out water through the sand
looking for clams in the ocean swells
But they also eat shrimp, crabs, tube worms, sea
cucumbers and other creatures
The walrus is a very distinctive animal with
many endearing features
Some people think they look funny with their
big tusks, moustaches and sweet faces
They spend half their life in the ocean and half
on land so they inhabit two places

## WANDERING SEA ANEMONE

The wandering sea anemone looks like a
ball of baked beans
Or you could see it as a beach ball or
even a bowl of jelly beans
These creatures usually are rooted to the
spot
But these wandering ones like to move
about a lot
They are such pretty colors that they keep
closed during the day
But out they come at night when they
want to eat and play
There are many brilliant colors gold,
yellow, white and pink
And many more besides these at least
that's what I think
You can find them in Australia or down
New Zealand way
Not even far out to sea but wandering
through a bay

## WHALE SHARK

The whale shark is the world's biggest
fish
And it's one of the most gentle as you
would wish
It is a huge creature up to 60 feet long
It can also weigh up to 60,000 tonnes
Though it has 3000 teeth they are very
tiny
It doesn't need them for feeding and
they're not spiny
Such a huge fish doesn't eat big fish it
eats tiny creatures
That is one of its most amazing features
Whale sharks are light brown with a white
underside
Sometimes they will let humans take a
ride
Each whale has a series of yellow dots
and stripes
Which work like our fingerprints day or
night
So if you know each whale shark's design
You can tell which one is swimming there
so fine

They float through the ocean like giant
Buddhas
With such a serene look on their face just
like garudas
They're not in a hurry as they can live for
100 years
As long as humans take care of them they
will have no fears

# WOBBEGONG

Wobbegongs look like your living room carpets
They swim on the bottom unlike other sharks
I wonder if one would lie on my floor
And create a lovely pattern by the back door
They are hairy and bobbly but have pretty whiskers
They don't usually bite us but will if we shift them
Some of them are spotty and some carry stripes
They wait for their prey and then quickly strike
Hidden in the sand they are the ambush king
To fool other fish their tail they'll swing
They have a huge mouth into which everything goes
All the other fish right down to their toes
A wobbegong shark you don't want for your mate
To be eaten by a carpet would be an awful fate

## XRAY FISH

You can see right through an Xray fish
You can see its bones and anything you
wish
An Xray fish can be quite scary
At least it's not really big and hairy
It would be a good companion on
Halloween
I bet it would make lots of people scream
But an Xray fish is peaceful and cool
And swims with its mates in a school
It's a kind fish with soft gentle eyes
And I'm sure it's also extremely wise

## YELLOW DOT GUARD CRAB

The yellow dot guard crab is like a little
soldier
Could there be another tiny creature
which is bolder
It protects the coral and guards it from
attack
The crab battles the crown of thorns
seastar and beats it back
The crab is only about half an inch in
length
But it has amazing courage and
impressive strength
The crown of thorns seastar is 12 inches
across
But the little crab does not let it be the
boss
In reefs which have the little guard crabs
The coral the seastar will not grab
Scientists are trying to introduce this little
soldier crab
To other reefs to protect them from
another snatch and grab

## YELLOWFIN TUNA

Yellowfin tuna are one of the fastest
swimmers in the ocean
They are also one of the strongest fish so
they always cause a commotion
Because of the way they breathe they can
never stop swimming
Throughout the night as well as all
through the day they keep skimming
Tuna it seems are very friendly with their
best mates the dolphins
They swim along together like two
friends who are golfing

## YELLOW MOUTH MORAY EEL

The yellow mouth moray eel never
squeals because it is very shy
In fact it doesn't even appear when the
sun is in the sky
It may seem like its bright yellow mouth
is meant to frighten
But the eel gets more of a fright so into
its cave it tightens
It's also called the starry eel because of its
star-spotted skin
But maybe it's also because during the
day it stays in
It may look ferocious when it opens its
canary yellow mouth
But it is simply trying to breathe in
oxygen from north or south
It's quite a gentle creature even though it
looks fierce
So you don't have to worry about this eel
your skin trying to pierce

## YERBURYI CHITON

Yerburyi Chiton look just like a baby's
cradle
You might see one as through the
shallows you wade
They bury themselves in coarse sand or
under rocks
If people don't know they're there they
might get a shock
They are a sea worm and their shell has
eight plates
If you invited one to dinner no doubt it
would be late
They eat algae and other organisms they
scrape with their gear
But very few creatures eat them so they
live for 40 years

## ZANZIBAR WHIP CORAL SHRIMP

The Zanzibar whip coral shrimp has its
own underwater cleaning station
And this very cute shrimp has a clever
way of attracting its patients
This hard-working shrimp waves its
antennas like a screen
So all the fish will know that it is ready to
clean
It's a pretty creature in orange yellow and
creamy white
Its cleaning station is open all day and all
night
This busy shrimp will clean inside and
outside a fish's mouth
It's not fussy so it cleans the fish from
north to south
These shrimp also make very good
housemates to other fish
For they keep their homes clean and
looking very swish

## ZEBRA DANIO

When a zebra danio falls in love, it's in
love for life
Once it has picked its mate, its mate is its
only wife
It's quite a strange concept for a tiny little
fish
To be as faithful as anyone could wish
A zebra danio is also a very playful fish
With its blue and gold stripes it's very
swish
It gets on well with others
And that includes its sisters and brothers
It's very good in schools
And also in freshwater pools
Originally from the mountains
But it also enjoys fountains

## ZIG ZAG COWRY

The cowry has a mantle that wraps
around its shell
It forms a jelly-like curtain that protects it
so well
It also can contract and shoot water
through its siphon
And then it can jet propel itself through
the water cycle
The beauty of the cowrie is there for all
to see
But it has also had a huge place in the
world's history
In China, India and Africa and all parts in
between
The cowrie was used as currency like a
regular Queen
For hundreds of years it was used just like
a piece of gold
In all of these many places in the
romantic years of old
For traders did not have money that was
made of paper or coin
So they came upon the solution in the
cowrie where it joins

And so the humble cowrie became a
worldwide help
To millions of people all over the world
its presence was felt

## THE COWFISH WHO JUMPED OVER THE MOON

One day a cowfish heard about a cow who jumped over the moon.

How did the cowfish hear about it, I can hear you ask. Well, I'll tell you.

A small child was swimming just above the coral reef where the cowfish lived and she distinctly heard the child say: "And the cow jumped over the moon".

The cowfish was very adventurous and so she decided that she too wanted to jump over the moon. But what was a moon? And what did it mean by jump, wondered the cowfish.

And I know you are wondering what was the cowfish' name. Well, I'll tell you. The cowfish' name was MOOOve Along Milky.

So MOOOve Along Milky, the cowfish, asked its friend the frogfish. "What is a moon and what does jump mean?"

The frogfish looked puzzled. "Not sure about a moon," she said. "But I can show you how to jump."

Now I know you are wondering what the frogfish' name was. Well, I'll tell you. The frogfish's name was Leaping Long-Legged Lenni.

And so Leaping Long-Legged Lenni, the frogfish, spent the afternoon on the reef showing MOOOve Along Milky, the cowfish, how to jump

Just then a moonfish happened along.

"What is a moon?" the cowfish – MOOOve Along Milky - asked the moonfish.

Now I just know that you are wondering what the name of the moonfish was. Well, I'll tell you. The moonfish's name was Moonbeam Melody Moonfish.

"A moon is a big golden light," said Moonbeam Melody Moonfish. "If you come swimming with me tonight I'll show you what a moon is."

So MOOOve Along Milky the cowfish went swimming with Moonbeam Melody Moonfish and Leaping Long-Legged Lenni the frogfish looked on.

But it was dark along the reef that night. There was no moon.

"I'm sorry," said Moonbeam Melody Moonfish. "We can try again tomorrow." MOOOve Along Milky the cowfish was sad. She so much wanted to jump right over the moon.

For seven nights the cowfish swam with the moonfish but for seven nights there was no moon.

But on the eighth night, as they swam along the reef, Moonbeam Melody Moonfish turned to MOOOve Along Milky the cowfish and said: "Tonight is your lucky night."

And just as she said that, MOOOve Along Milky the cowfish could see a big round bright yellow light shining onto the reef.

"That's the moon," said the moonfish. And as the moonfish and the frogfish watched, the cowfish did a huge leap and jumped right over the moon, just as she had wanted.

## THE SOFTLY SPOKEN SHARK

The softly-spoken shark was so very sad. His hiss and his snap and his bite were too gentle for anyone to take any notice of him.

'How will I ever be a feared and ferocious fish if no-one notices me,' he thought. Such a sad sob escaped his mouth but it was so soft that it was not heard by anyone.

No-one, that is, except for Petranella Porpoise. Petranella had a big heart – some fish said her heart was as big as a whale's heart but I think they were exaggerating a bit.

Petranella hated to see any sea creature unhappy so she asked the softly-spoken shark – whose name was Stupenda Shark – why he was so sad. And the softly-spoken shark –Stupenda – sighed again and softly started to tell Petranella Porpoise about his troubles.

"A shark should be ferocious and feared," he softly said.

"But no-one takes any notice of me, why

they don't even hear me," he sobbed.
"I am a failure as a shark. I am too soft."
Petranella Porpoise could see Stupenda's
perceived problem. She swam up close to
him and said:
"Stupenda, it all depends on your point of
view."
"What do you mean?" asked Stupenda,
his curiosity aroused.
"Just because you are a shark, it doesn't
automatically follow that you have to be
ferocious and feared."
"Well all the sharks I know are ferocious
and feared," said Stupenda, the softly-
spoken shark.
"But there are many, many sharks in the
ocean. Do you know all of them?"
"No," said Stupenda. " I suppose I don't
know all of them."
"If you knew that a shark was huge – I
mean really big – would you think that
that shark would be ferocious and
feared?" asked Petranella Porpoise.
"Certainly I would," said the softly-
spoken shark, Stupenda.
"Now if you knew of a shark that was so

big it was called a whale shark would you think it was a ferocious and feared shark?" asked Stupenda.

"Certainly, of course and definitely," said Stupenda, getting quite excited. "That would be a very ferocious shark indeed and tremendously feared."

Petranella Porpoise smiled at the softly-spoken shark. "Oh, you think so? Well in actual fact there is a whale shark in the ocean and it is a very gentle and softly spoken fish, not a bit ferocious and certainly not feared."

Well, Stupenda the softly-spoken shark was astounded. A shark so big it was called a whale shark and yet it was a gentle creature and was very softly-spoken.

So Stupenda thanked Petranella Porpoise and he swam away supremely satisfied that he was just as he should be – a softly-spoken shark.

# THE MAN WHO HAD A WISH
## TO BE A FISH

There was once a man who loved to swim in the ocean. He would come down to the seashore very, very early in the morning and he would start swimming. He loved the way the ocean felt as he swam, he felt more at home in the ocean than he did on the land.

He would swim all day long until the sun finally sank softly into the ocean like a sliding fried egg.

When it was so dark that he couldn't see the seashore any more, he would slowly climb out of the water and reluctantly go home.

Until the next day and as soon as the dawn light started to slip its feathery fingers across the sun the man would slip on his swimmers and slide right down to the water's edge and slip happily into the ocean and spend another day swimming. He never got hungry when he was in the ocean.

He almost felt like the ocean fed him through the pores in his skin as he was swimming. He came to know the ocean creatures so well that he had names for them all. Every day some of the ocean creatures would come and visit him while he swam and eventually he had a huge family of ocean creatures and he began to feel that they were more his family than the people he had left behind on the land in his house.

One day while he was swimming he felt as if it was no effort at all to swim. It was as if he could swim like a fish. And he even began to feel like a fish. Finally at the end of the day when he reluctantly climbed out onto the seashore from the ocean, he looked down at his feet and he noticed something. They did not look like his feet anymore. There were little webs in between his toes.

I wonder if I am turning into a fish, he thought. And he was very happy at the thought that that might be exactly what was happening. He had often wished that he had been born as a fish.

Maybe his wish to be a fish was coming
true.

The next day when the man was
swimming in the ocean his arms started
to feel lighter than they had ever felt
before and it was even easier for him to
swim than it had been the day before.
And, as he swam, he looked at his arms
and he could see that they looked
different. His arms seemed to be growing
scales on them and they were beginning
to look like the fins of a fish.

Now some people might have been
extremely worried if their arms started to
grow scales but not this man. He was
happy indeed because he felt that at last
his wish to be a fish was actually going to
come true.

'I wonder,' he thought. 'I wonder how
long it will be before I will be a true fish
and then I can swim all night as well as all
day.'

Well, he didn't have long to find out.
Because the very next day as he was
swimming, his whole body started to
grow scales.

And the day after that his eyes started to change into fish eyes and he could see all around him – even behind his head.

The day after that his hair fell out and then scales began to grow on his head.

''Well,' thought the man. 'I guess I don't need to go home anymore. I can just stay in this beautiful ocean and swim all night as well as all day.' And that is exactly what he did.

And do you know what that man's name was?

Well, I'll tell you.

The man who had a wish to be a fish was called Mr Fisher.

# ABOUT THE AUTHOR

## Sally Squires

**PO Box 37126**
**Honolulu HI 96837**

GDay1717@hotmail.com
ssquires1717@gmail.com

www.gdaysally.com
www.nusefuse.com
www.typhoontreasures.com
www.messagefromamermaid.com

Sally Squires is an Australian writer, director and producer, who moved to New York in 1997. She won an award for writing a documentary in Singapore and has written many children's stories including The Mouse Who Danced at Covent Garden, which was made into a TV show and a radio serial and which is the first chapter of her children's book "Micetralia". Sally makes short films, documentaries and features and has a weekly TV show, Metro Elvis, which is broadcast in New York and Honolulu and is also on her vimeo channel: www.vimeo.com/metroelvis. She also has a weekly radio show called the G'Day Sally Show in which she reads stories and poems for children and in which she advocates for conservation. (**www.kwai1080am.com**) KWAI 1080 AM SATURDAY 7PM

Sally also writes feature film scripts, plays, comedy, novels, poetry, short stories and song lyrics. Her poems have been published in American Poetry Anthologies. She has produced several short films, a half hour children's TV show called "Wizzo Bizzo Gizzmos" and several half hour TV specials.

One of her feature film scripts set in New York, "Declaration of Peace", was chosen for a directed screenplay reading and she has written several other feature film scripts.

Sally directed and produced two feature length documentaries: "The Day The Sky Fell" on the World Trade Center events and "Did You Ever Have a Dream" about P-Funk, a brilliant disabled musician who lives in Harlem. She was also assistant director and associate producer on the feature film "The Situation" which won best feature film at Martha's Vineyard African American Film Festival in 2006 and which has been showcased at film festivals across the country.

Her novel "Napoleon's Last Night" was chosen as a finalist in the William Wisdom-William Faulkner awards in 2010.

# Sally's books: (**www.gdaysally.com**)

<u>FOR ADULTS:</u>

Dragon Weaver
Skin of the Kangaroo
Alligators and Jack Nicholson
Napoleon's Last Night
Saucy Sally's Salubrious Scrummies
G'Day Mate

<u>FOR CHILDREN:</u>
Dragonfly Diary
The Story Tree
Mermaids Are Cool
Micetralia
Angels With Attitude
NICK NACK NOCK
OZZ WOZZ

The updated version of her 9/11 film "The Day
The Sky Fell 2010 The Sky Is Rising" is also
available online

Sally is also committed to raising funds for girls in Nepal to give them education scholarships. You can help support her in this endeavor by sending a donation to her paypal account:
**GDay1717@hotmail.com**

You can also support her children's radio show by donating to:
www.gofundme.com/gdaysallyshow

87566666R00137

Made in the USA
Columbia, SC
23 January 2018